Best Wishes

[signature]

Final Voyages

Final Voyages

Volume I

by

Jim Wellman

Flanker Press Ltd.
St. John's, NL
2003

National Library of Canada Cataloguing in Publication

Wellman, Jim, 1946-
    Final voyages / by Jim Wellman.

Stories originally published in The Navigator, 1997-2003.
ISBN 1-894463-43-9 (v. 1)

    1. Fisheries--Accidents--Atlantic Coast (Canada)--Anecdotes.
2. Fishing boats--Atlantic Coast (Canada)--Anecdotes. 3. Shipwrecks--
Atlantic Coast (Canada)--Anecdotes. I. Title. II. Title: Navigator (St.
John's, Nfld.)

VK1275.A856W44 2003   363.11'963922'09715   C2003-905486-1

Copyright © 2003 by Jim Wellman

PRINTED IN CANADA BY FRIESENS CORPORATION

First printing November 2003
Second printing January 2004
Third printing June 2005

Flanker Press Ltd.
P.O. Box 2522, Station C
St. John's, NL A1C 6K1
Toll Free: 1-866-739-4420
Telephone: (709) 739-4477
Fax: (709) 739-4420

E-mail: info@flankerpress.com
www.flankerpress.com

Dedication

This book is dedicated to the families of the thousands of fishermen in Atlantic Canada who lost their lives at sea in the pursuit of earning a living from the northwest Atlantic Ocean.

Acknowledgements

A Sincere Thank You to:

All the women and men who courageously allowed me to invade their privacy and so generously recounted for me the most painful times of their lives.

The publishers of *The Navigator* magazine. From day one, TriNav Directors Paul Pinhorn, Trevor Decker and Rick Young encouraged me to publish "Final Voyages" as a book.

Stephanie Moore – graphic arts designer with *The Navigator* magazine for her ingenuity in the creation of the cover for this book.

And – to the readers of *The Navigator* who have made "Final Voyages" one of the most popular features of the "Voice of the fishing industry in Atlantic Canada."

– Jim Wellman

Table of Contents

Introduction

Fishing has long been documented as being the most dangerous occupation in the world. That is especially true in the harsh, and often bitter, marine environment of Atlantic Canada.

The report of the Royal Commission on the sinking of the drill rig *Ocean Ranger* in 1982 stated:

> "There are few areas in the world which possess as severe environmental conditions as the continental shelf off eastern Canada. Nowhere else are the combinations of wind, wave, fog and ice as perilous and unpredictable as in that vast and varied expanse of ocean."

Those perilous conditions have caused the sinking and loss of hundreds of Atlantic Canadian fishing vessels, claiming enormous loss of life.

Fishing families in towns like Grand Bank, Burin, Twillingate, Lunenburg, Bonavista, Yarmouth and Glace Bay have too often suffered the pain of losing husbands, fathers, brothers and sons to the ocean that, ironically, also provided those same men and their families its great bounty of riches.

Former host of CBC Radio's *Fisheries Broadcast* and now managing editor of *The Navigator,* Jim Wellman recounts some of those gripping tales as part of his regular monthly feature in *The Navigator,* an Atlantic Canadian fisheries publication.

Wellman has restricted his stories to incidents involving small/inshore vessels using the federal government's standard of less than 65 feet in length as the definition of "inshore."

Dubbed "Final Voyages," the feature has been one of the most popular sections of *The Navigator* since the magazine's first issue in December 1997.

Ocean Claims Well-Known Fisherman

The Troake family of Twillingate had everything well-planned for Thanksgiving dinner in October 2000.

Florence Troake would attend church service on Thanksgiving Sunday morning, October 8, while her husband, Jack, would stay home and cook dinner for the entire Troake clan. Children, grandchildren, nephews, nieces and in-laws would start arriving at Jack and Florence's house between 12:30 and 1:00 P.M. to carry on a longstanding family Thanksgiving tradition. After all, the Troakes had much to be thankful for. Jack, a very successful fishermen/sealer, and Florence lived comfortably in their modest two-storey home in Twillingate, and life for the rest of the family was going along just fine for the most part.

Their son Gary Troake hadn't missed Thanksgiving dinner with his parents in years and, although he had things to tend to, he didn't plan to miss this one either. Also on the list of family invites was 32-year-old Roger Blake who had married their granddaughter Dana Troake just three months previously.

Gary was one of the best-known fishermen in Newfoundland and Labrador. Intelligent and well-read, Gary was a visionary. He was also a passionate debater about the culture of his chosen vocation as a sealer and fisherman.

As a sealer, Gary was perhaps the industry's best spokesperson, always presenting a compelling and convincing case in support of the seal harvest, while at the same time always stressing the urgent need to focus on long-term conservation strategies for all marine animals. Because of his gift as a very articulate communicator, Gary was often the featured speaker or panellist at numerous seminars, workshops and meetings dealing with sealing and the fisheries. He worked tirelessly to improve the image of the sealing industry. In the days when the heated controversy over the seal hunt attracted media from all over the world, mainland and foreign correspondents often mistook Gary for an animal-rights protestor from central Canada or the United States. Along with his beard, his long hair usually worn in a braided ponytail made him look more like their idea of a seal-hunt protestor than a Newfoundland sealer.

On Saturday night, October 7, 2000, 40-year-old Gary Troake was working at a few odds and ends in his gear shed when his friend David Boyd dropped by. David, a former teacher turned fisherman, always loved to chat with Gary. The two of them talked endlessly about why the northern cod fishery collapsed and how to prevent the same thing from occurring with other species.

Saturday night's conversation was no different. Before heading to their respective houses nearby, Gary mentioned that he had to go out and take in his gill nets on Sunday morning. A government regulation at the time prohibited fishermen from leaving gill nets in the

Twillingate.

water on Sundays. Gary had gone out earlier that day to retrieve his nets, but high winds and rough seas prevented him from getting more than three or four. As the two men were leaving the gear shed to go home, David noted that the weather had not improved and urged Gary that it was not safe to go out again on Sunday morning. Gary mentioned something about not wanting to have his nets confiscated by Department of Fisheries and Oceans (DFO) officers if they saw them in the water, but said that he'd make up his mind in the morning.

On Sunday morning, Gary chatted with his father, Jack. Once again he worried about what would happen if fisheries enforcement officers seized his nets.

"He knew the weather was bad and I didn't want him to go. I told him that it was a lousy rotten regulation anyway and that there were probably so many other nets still in the water because of the bad weather that the DFO fellas would say to hell with it and give up on it anyway," Jack says.

Gary knew his father was probably right, but his fear of having so many nets taken from him weighed heavily on his mind. In the end his fear of losing the nets overruled and he decided to go – after all, it would be an hour or so and he'd be back again, he told himself. He called Roger Blake with his decision, and the two men were heading out from Twillingate Harbour by 10:45 A.M. with a promise to be back in plenty of time for Thanksgiving dinner.

The two fishermen were seen just before 11:30 A.M. hauling a couple of their nets that were located close to the harbour entrance before they headed to Shag Rocks where most of their nets were set.

Looking out over the harbour from his living room window, Jack Troake was restless. He knew that Gary and Roger only had a short steam to Shag Rocks, but it was windy and the seas were high. As a veteran fishermen Jack knew almost exactly how long it would take to get around Long Point to Shag Rocks given the northwest winds and the state of the sea. From the location where they were observed at eleven-thirty, Shag Rocks would have been about 15 to 20 minutes away in their 19-foot fibreglass speedboat.

Thanksgiving dinner was cooking and Jack was sitting at the kitchen table when he suddenly became overwhelmed with a strong sense of foreboding.

"I jumped up from the table and went to the closet to get my coat – I was going to drive down to Long Point and see if I could see the boys. I didn't hear any voice or anything like that, but something was telling me that Gary was in trouble, you know," he says. But Jack stopped when he reached the clothes closet door. "I looked at the clock and thought to myself 'I can't go out now – it's ten after twelve and the crowd are just about ready to start in coming.'" Telling himself that he was just simply too worried, he shook off his initial strange sensation and went back to the kitchen, reassuring himself that Gary and Roger would back in a half hour or so.

The family members all arrived as planned, but Jack Troake was not hungry. All through dinner he kept a close eye on the clock and grew increasingly agitated when there was still no sign of Gary and Roger.

"I didn't finish my dinner, but I couldn't hold off any longer – around one o'clock, I got my coat and went to the truck," he says. Driving up Long Point hill toward the lighthouse, Jack looked to the northwest where he could see Shag Rocks.

He didn't need to look any farther.

Gary's overturned boat was in plain view, but there was no sign of Gary or Roger.

"And that's the hardest part," Jack says today, his voice quivering. "If I had gone up at ten after twelve, I wonder if I might have found him alive – it's awful hard to live with that feeling now."

A half hour later, searchers, most of them close friends of Gary Troake, were in the area searching for the two fishermen. Gary

Greenham brought his boat as close as he could to the swamped speedboat, but after circling around a couple of times he saw nothing. Although his logic was telling him to move on and look elsewhere, his sixth sense kept saying that he should give it another try. On his third or fourth manoeuvre, Gary Greenham's worst fears were realized. Gary Troake's lifeless body floated out from underneath the overturned boat.

Jack Troake figures he has a pretty fair idea of what happened. The propeller of the 40-horsepower outboard motor was severely damaged from what appeared to be hitting rocks. Jack thinks the wind and waves pushed the boat too close to a rocky shoal known as Evil Rock, and in Gary's attempts to clear the shoal, a large wave came crashing across them, swamping the boat.

Gary Troake tied himself to a net buoy with a rope. Roger Blake didn't and, subsequently, his body was never recovered.

One of the largest funerals in Twillingate was held on October 11, 2000 when hundreds of people turned out to say goodbye and wish Gary Troake well on his *final voyage*.

One of them was Gary's friend David Boyd who wrote a poem for the occasion:

"Eagles Fly Alone"

The vulture and the carrion crow
Steal scraps from the lion's bone.
But the eagle soars above the flock,
Cause eagles fly alone!

Tho' crowds condemn and criticize
With words in angry tone.
You always found some good to say,
Cause eagles fly alone!

A kitten from its mother strayed,
A young girl far from home.
While others passed you took them in,
Cause eagles fly alone!

It mattered not a person's rank,
On the streets or on a throne.
You gave respect as you felt due,
Cause eagles fly alone!

Brutal Test of Endurance on Labrador Sea Ice

"The nights were endless."

That's how Garland Curl, George Brown and Clifford Curl remember the longest week of their lives.

The first day of May 1982 started out routinely enough for the three fishermen from Fox Harbour-St. Lewis, Labrador, but a quick trip to hunt a few seals turned out to be a brutal test of courage and endurance for the three friends.

It was foggy and there were a lot of ice floes near Fox Harbour on Saturday morning, but Garland, Clifford and George didn't worry about that when they headed toward Cape Lewis in Garland's speedboat. This was going to be barely more than a pleasure-ride with a plan to get two or three seals and return home by lunch hour.

When morning ended the trio had taken six seals along with a few dozen saltwater birds known locally as turrs. Satisfied with their take, the men decided to head home at approximately 12:30 P.M. Garland didn't carry a compass in his small 18-foot boat and extremely thick fog made it impossible to see the sun. Without a reference point for directions, the three fishermen had to guess which way to go. After steaming three hours in what should have been less than an hour's boat-ride, they realized that they had guessed incorrectly.

By six o'clock Saturday evening, the ice pans had become closely packed together and manoeuvring the small boat had become difficult. Hearing no sounds that indicated land was nearby, they decided to pull the boat up on an ice pan and spend the night in hopes that Sunday morning would dawn a better day.

To protect themselves from the cold, freezing drizzle, the men turned the small speedboat bottom up and built a makeshift shelter underneath it using the turrs as a mattress to sit on. Breaking an oar and gathering pieces of other wood they splintered from the speedboat's hull, the men managed to light a fire and kept it smoldering all night by adding pieces of rope.

"Even without food or sleep, Saturday was a real comfortable night compared to what we were about to face," Garland remembers.

Unfortunately, conditions had not improved by daylight Sunday morning. It was still cold and damp in drizzle and thick fog. The only

Ship skeleton.

change was for the worse. The ice floes had become totally packed together making it impossible to use the boat – walking would be the only way out of there. Sometime during the early morning, the fog lifted long enough that the men could see land. Peering across what seemed like endless ice fields, the men estimated that they were at least 20 miles from the coast. Knowing that it would take a couple of days to make it across the ice to the Labrador coastline on foot, the men decided to store up some energy by eating a seabird. One of them hooked a skinned turr on a gaff and held it over a small fire that the others had managed to build from the few remaining pieces of wood and rope.

"What a hard-looking sight that bird was," Garland recalls, laughing. "He was coal-black and tough as a rubber boot. We had a hard time getting it down. I kept thinking that if only I had a bit of salt on it, it wouldn't be too bad, but it was hard to take," he says.

As George and Clifford packed a few things in their knapsacks, Garland nailed a note to the boat telling possible rescuers that they were fine and had left to walk to land. That way, if searchers found the boat they would know to look for men walking on the ice instead of assuming that all three had drowned.

Walking over rough sea-ice off Labrador is not a Sunday stroll in the park. Besides having to be constantly wary of thin ice that, when covered with snow, can look deceptively like solid thick ice, there were huge clumps of high rafted floes that made walking nearly impossible at times.

"Sometimes, we'd walk a mile to gain a hundred feet," Garland says. Still, they were determined as they plodded on until darkness fell about seven-thirty on Sunday evening. Unable to even sit on the cold ice, the three had no choice but to keep walking around in circles in the dark, sometimes huddling together to keep warm until daylight.

Early Monday morning the men managed to get another glimpse through the ever-present fog and drizzle and although they caught sight of land, there was little reason for celebration. They suddenly realized that despite walking nearly all day on Sunday, they were still just as far offshore as they were 24 hours ago.

"The tide and currents off Labrador always run south and east and we had drifted on the ice back to more or less where we were on Sunday morning," Garland explains.

Although cold, wet, hungry, tired and, by now, extremely thirsty, Garland Curl, George Brown and Clifford Curl knew they had no options. They simply had to keep walking and hope and pray that somehow they would manage to reach land. For a few moments on Monday evening they felt their long days of trudging across endless ice floes had paid off. In the distance they could hear the unmistakable sound of an airplane. Knowing that the only sustained airplane activity around St. Lewis would be a search plane, the three men felt a surge of hope run through their veins. But when the sounds didn't come any closer, the men realized that the planes had set a search grid in the area where they killed their seals on Saturday morning, nearly 20 miles away.

As darkness fell that night, the men felt more dejected than before they heard the sound of planes. Although they said nothing, all three once again started their dreaded nightly ritual of walking in circles, each of them silently wondering if the search coordinators would broaden their search plan to come farther offshore.

To ease their hunger pains, the men tried eating several hearts of the turrs they had packed in their knapsacks on Sunday. George and Garland managed to digest a few of the raw hearts, but even though he was aware of the importance of food as an energy source in those circumstances, Clifford simply couldn't swallow the raw meat without throwing it back up again.

When daylight broke on Tuesday morning, George and Garland were both still in surprisingly good condition but Clifford was beginning to weaken. The effects of three days without food and water were also gravely aggravated when Clifford fell through the ice into the bitterly cold water. Soaked clothes and boots full of freezing water did nothing to help matters, although he somehow managed to plod on alongside his friends, trying desperately to get a little closer to land.

George had a taste of what Clifford was going through. Although he hadn't fallen through into the water, his boots had also become soaked and each step he took was in wet and nearly frozen socks. Garland, luckily, had managed to stay dry. Attempting to help his buddies, Garland cut the legs off his long johns and tore the sleeves from his sweater and wrapped the material around his friends' feet. It helped for a while but soon the cold water in their boots had soaked through to the skin and soon they were both once again in agonizing discomfort.

As the three men continued to walk all day Tuesday, they could hear the drone of an aircraft searching up and down the Labrador coastline, but never coming offshore near them. They killed a seal and tried igniting the fat from the animal to start a fire. Although they burned all the remaining fuel in their three disposable cigarette lighters, the fat would not ignite.

Tuesday evening, things got even worse. The ice pans were separated by the ocean currents and suddenly they were stranded on a single piece of ice. The last shred of control that they might have had over their own fate was now stripped away from them.

Drifting helplessly on a 30- by 50-foot ice pan on the Labrador Sea, shrouded in drizzle and fog without shelter, food or water was as depressing and as unbearable as life could get.

After three days and nights of continuous walking over ice floes trying to get closer to land, Garland Curl, George Brown and

Clifford Curl couldn't believe their bad luck as darkness fell. Instead of getting closer to home, the men found themselves floating helplessly farther offshore. They were also drifting away from hopes of survival.

Although the men hadn't eaten in three days, the constant hunger pains started to subside on Tuesday, but their thirst for water would not go away. Sometimes they would put ice on their parched lips to ease the discomfort but the saltwater ice probably made things worse. "We desperately longed for something to drink, especially for something warm to take the chill from our bodies," Garland says. But there was no hot chocolate, there was no cold water, there was no food and there was no escaping the harsh reality that if help didn't arrive soon, death was inevitable within days.

As long as they were on solid ice there was hope that, even against formidable odds, they might make it to land. But now their fears raced to new heights. Now they faced the possibility that the ice pan they were on would split into pieces, separating them from each other or even worse, it might roll over, throwing them all into the freezing Labrador Sea. Trudging round and round in endless circles in the fog and freezing mist, the three men worried about what they would do if winds increased, or if a storm came up. They worried too about their families who, by now, had probably given them up for dead. They knew that without food and water they would soon weaken and suffer from hypothermia. *Who would die first – what would the others do if one of them gave up – who would be the last to go?* they wondered, silently.

About eleven o'clock on Wednesday night they stopped worrying for a few minutes. In the distance they could hear the drone of engines. They first thought that it might have been an airplane, but soon recognized the unmistakable sound of an approaching ship. Surges of energy and joy coursed through their bodies when they saw the lights of an icebreaker coming towards them through the fog.

Knowing their chances of rescue would be better if they could send a signal in the dark night, Garland took a shotgun shell from his pocket, broke it open and quickly packed the gunpowder around the wheel of his cigarette lighter. There was no fuel in the lighter but he hoped the spark from the flint would ignite the powder and create enough light to attract the attention of the ship's crew. Reminded by his friends that the gunpowder might explode in his face, Garland simply shrugged.

"What odds, at least you two will be saved," he replied, working to prepare the powder properly. While all three yelled as loudly as they could, Garland constantly flicked the wheel of the lighter, but the powder would not ignite and the Coast Guard ship *Jackman* steamed past them stealthily into the darkness like a thief in the night.

"That's when it started to hurt real bad," Garland recalls, shaking his head quietly. "They were no more than three or four hundred feet away from us – we could see the men on the bridge, they were that close – if we'd been on solid ice we could have run over and thrown something at them to attract their attention."

Watching the wake of a rescue ship fade into the black night brought the stranded men to new depths of despair. Fighting depression was difficult that night, but somehow they managed to stay on their feet knowing that if they stopped to lie down for a rest, they would not wake up again.

Thursday morning dawned with a small ray of hope for the weakening men. The winds had shifted to a southwesterly flow, bringing slightly drier air over the Labrador Sea. The fog lifted long enough to allow Clifford, George and Garland to get a good view of their surroundings. To their surprise and dismay, the ice had drifted so far offshore that the Labrador landscape was barely visible on the horizon.

But despite their location, the fog-free conditions gave their spirits another much-needed boost. In the distance, they could see a helicopter flying directly towards them.

"It was coming at us as straight as you could draw a line from the land to where we were standing," Garland says. As the chopper drew nearer, all three began waving their arms and doing whatever else they could to make sure they wouldn't be missed again.

It didn't work. Amazingly, the helicopter flew directly over their heads and, as the pilot and crew scanned the water and ice floes on either side of the aircraft, none of them saw the men frantically waving just a few feet directly below them on the ice pan. As the chopper sped away into the distance, Garland, George and Clifford stood still and stared in shocked amazement. How many times could rescue come so close only to elude them as if teasing their sanity? they wondered. To make matters worse, the fog rolled back in again and when the helicopter turned around and headed back to land, it was so thick that the three men could only hear the sound of the chopper as it passed once again almost directly overhead.

Discouraged by such a long list of bitter disappointments, Clifford decided that he couldn't go on any longer. Soaked and chilled to the bones, he told his companions that he was giving up and was going to lie down for a rest. Aware that "lying down for a rest," meant dying, George and Garland discussed what they should do next. They both knew that the likelihood of rescue was growing dim, yet they were not ready to give up.

"It was Thursday morning and we said we'd hang on till Sunday before we'd go," Garland says, talking casually, as if they were making a decision on a routine family outing.

Shortly after noon on Thursday the fog lifted for the second time that day and, once again, the men could see several miles in the distance. At first they couldn't believe their eyes, but there was a ship located about four miles to the south of them. Although the vessel was not heading in their direction, Garland and George were not going to let another chance at rescue get away without trying to do the best they could to attract attention. Finding the highest clump on the ice pan that had become home to the men, Garland climbed to the top and took off his orange rain gear and started swinging it in circles above his head.

After several minutes of waving his jacket, Garland saw the boat turning around. Afraid of letting his hopes grow for fear of another letdown, Garland kept on waving the jacket in the air until he thought they might have been spotted.

"When I saw a big puff of smoke coming out of her stack, I figured they'd seen something." This time, he was right. A woman on watch on the bridge of the Coast Guard vessel *Wolfe* had been scanning the ice floes through her binoculars and saw Garland's orange coat waving from the tip of the ice pan.

With the news that a rescue ship was approaching, Clifford, lying on the ice, suddenly felt a renewed energy flowing through his body. When the *Wolfe* slowed alongside, he was just as lively as his two buddies.

To the astonishment of the crew aboard the rescue ship, the three men, who had been stranded on ice for five days without food or water, were able to climb the rope ladder unaided, up and over the side of the ship.

Safe on board the *Wolfe*, Garland, George and Clifford were served tea mixed with brandy. "It was the best thing I'd ever tasted in all my life," says Garland, smiling at the memory. "But we couldn't eat, as much as the crew tried to feed us, we just couldn't get anything down."

Back on land, the men were given immediate medical attention. Garland, who remained dry throughout the ordeal, was fine. Clifford, who seemed at first to have suffered the worst effects, was also in surprisingly good condition overall and, like Garland, he was doing routine jobs around the house the next day. Although George appeared to be in good condition to the end, he had suffered serious damage to a foot that had frozen. He required medical attention for several weeks. But still, considering the unbelievable hardships of those five days, Garland Curl, George Brown and Clifford Curl survived incredible odds and escaped what was perilously close to being their *final voyage*.

Routine Fishing Trip Ends Tragically

Howard Hobbs is 72.

The retired fisherman from Keels in Bonavista Bay, NL is happy to tell you that he's never spent a day in hospital in all his years, but he and his wife have had more than their share of heartaches.

Almost 30 years ago on August 31, 1973 their 12-year-old daughter stopped by the Bonavista Cold Storage fish plant in Bonavista as she played in the area with friends. Someone in the plant gave the young girls a ride in the elevator, but young Ruby was so curious about elevators she decided to go back alone and give it a try all by herself. The old-fashioned style equipment had a gate that opened before a person could step into the elevator car. No one is sure what happened, but it seems that perhaps Ruby didn't operate the gate properly, or maybe she pushed the start/stop buttons more than once, but something went horribly wrong and the young girl got snagged under the gate as it closed. Within minutes, she succumbed from the injuries she sustained.

Today, Howard Hobbs remembers that evening as if were just yesterday, but these days he has fresher and equally painful memories. He and his wife are still grieving over the loss of a son and grandson in 2001. Boyd Hobbs was 44 years old and a respected fisherman.

When Howard starts to talk about Boyd's fishing abilities, for a moment, there is a smile and a chuckle.

"He caught 3,000 pounds of fish one day on hook and line. Now sir, that's some pullin' over the gunwale isn't it? He used five buckets of bait, can you imagine that? He had sore fingers the next day, but that didn't bother him much," Howard says, smiling proudly, remembering his son fondly.

The smile fades quickly, though, when Howard recalls the events of July 24, 2001.

The day started like most other July days for inshore crab fishermen in Bonavista. It was a lovely summer day with just a slight breeze – almost as good as it gets for fishing in Newfoundland waters. Inshore crab fishermen were up bright and early taking advantage of the weather to haul and set their fishing gear. Boyd Hobbs, his 18-year-old son Darryl and a friend and crew member, 28-year-old Darryl Clements, originally from Petty Harbour, were among those heading out that morning.

The steam to the crab grounds, about 17 to 20 miles off Bonavista, went well for the three men in their 22-foot boat. Several vessels of different shapes and sizes were busy hauling and setting crab pots all morning.

Not far from Boyd Hobbs's boat, his friend Bob Hayward was having trouble with his crab hauler. Around 2:00 P.M., Boyd offered to haul the rest of Bob's pots before finishing up for the day.

"You might as well go on in out of it, because there's nothing you can do out here now anyway," Boyd said to Bob. Part of Boyd's plan was to keep several crab pots on board and move them to crab grounds nearer to shore. Depending on weather, he might have done that later the same evening or the next day – either way he'd be heading toward Bonavista shortly after Bob left to go home.

It wasn't sudden, but the wind freshened from the west-southwest fairly quickly about four o'clock, just as most boats were on the way back to port. By six o'clock the winds had strengthened considerably.

After supper, when word started to trickle around Bonavista that Boyd Hobbs, his son Darryl and Darryl Clements hadn't arrived back in port, many fishermen grew very concerned because, by then, the winds were near storm force. A little later, a couple of longliners decided to take a look outside the harbour area before darkness fell. When they returned with the news that they hadn't seen any sign of the three men, a very sombre pall settled over the fishing town.

At midnight, Howard Hobbs's phone rang. It was his son Clayton saying, "Boyd and Darryl didn't get in this evening." A veteran fisherman and man of the ocean, Howard didn't need much time to realize that surviving a windstorm of such force in a small 22-foot open boat was almost impossible.

"Boy, they're gone then," Howard said softly to Clayton. "Let's go down and see what's going on." A few minutes later Howard and Clayton were on the road from Keels to nearby Bonavista.

Going directly to the wharf, Howard remembers being surprised at how many people were there, considering the lateness of the hour.

"They were lined off around the wharf. There were cars and trucks everywhere," he says. There were boats already out searching and others at the wharf staying in constant radio contact with those who were out to pass on any news if something happened.

There was nothing to report.

Discouraged and dejected, a tired Howard Hobbs went back home to Keels at 3:00 A.M., but after resting just a few hours he was back in Bonavista again keeping lookout from the famous cape where John Cabot is said to have made landfall more than 500 years before.

Coast Guard ships combed the ocean and Search and Rescue (SAR) helicopters scanned the sea from the air. After searching for a week, covering 7,000 square kilometres of ocean surface, there was no sign of bodies; not even a trace of debris was found.

Howard remembers standing on Cape Bonavista near the lighthouse during the second day of search efforts. He watched a SAR helicopter circling the area near the cape, staring at it, as well as keeping an eye on the dark waters below, as if he was part of the search team on board the chopper. His concentration was broken when a man got out of a car with Alberta licence plates and walked up to Howard saying, "what a waste of taxpayers' money, having those government helicopters out there flying around like that."

A soft-spoken man, Howard looked at the man and said quietly, "I don't think so, sir, they're searching for my boys – my son and my grandson who are lost out there," pointing to the still-wild ocean. The man was extremely apologetic and quickly left Howard to maintain his vigil in peace.

No one will ever know whether the three men had left the fishing grounds or if they might have made it almost to the harbour entrance when they were obviously swamped and/or capsized. Many fishermen, including Howard, feel the 22-foot boat was incapable of handling very high winds and seas, especially with a load of crab pots on board. Equipped with a 20-horsepower diesel, inboard engine, the boat might have sunk straight to the bottom with the overwhelming weight of even one large wave crashing over it.

As usual when there are no bodies recovered and not even a single clue found to help understand or confirm what happened to allow for some sort of closure, dealing with such a tragic loss is still difficult for the families.

Only one thing is certain, Boyd Hobbs, his 18-year-old son Darryl along with 28-year-old Darryl Clements made their *final voyage* on July 24, 2001.

Near-Tragedy Had Light Moments

On November 30, 1989, skipper Bob Truckair and his five-man crew left Glace Bay, Nova Scotia on what was expected to be a routine two- or three-day fishing trip to the Cape North area of Cape Breton. As the *Musn't Tell* slipped from the harbour around noon that day, there was a moderate breeze on her port bow, but the forecast didn't call for weather conditions that the 65-foot inshore dragger couldn't handle.

While there was nothing to fear from a safety standpoint, the weather out at the cape was unsuitable for comfortable dragging, so the 41-year-old skipper decided to ride it out and wait until seas and winds improved before shooting away the nets. As expected, the weather did improve the next night and on the morning of December 2, the *Musn't Tell* steamed offshore to the edge of the fishing grounds. Fishing went well throughout the afternoon and after three tows the crew had hauled back about 100,000 pounds of fish. During the tows, Bob had brief conversations with the skippers of two larger draggers fishing in the area. The *Zion* out of Newfoundland, owned by Fishery Products International, and the *Cape York* out of Lunenburg, Nova Scotia were also doing well, and by late afternoon all three vessels had wound up on Smokey Bank, southwest of Cape North.

The crew of the *Musn't Tell* took back the last tow just as darkness fell, so Bob decided that after they had put the gear away they would head to Glace Bay, only 18 miles away. When they started to steam toward home, Bob phoned his wife to tell her that he'd be in around midnight and wondered if she'd mind cooking him dinner, because he was hungry for a home-cooked meal.

Shortly after Bob's call, Walter Dominic came up from the galley and said that he could take over on the wheel, suggesting that Bob should get a rest on the way in. That was when Bob noticed something was not quite right with the dragger.

"Walter, there's something wrong with this boat tonight," Bob said. An experienced fisherman from Rose Blanche in Newfoundland and mate on the *Musn't Tell*, Walter carefully checked the engine room, the lazarette, fish hold, and engine room, but saw nothing out of the ordinary – there was no buildup of water.

"I don't know what it is then but she's not coming all the way back from the port side after listing in a swell," Bob said to Walter. There was a 25-knot northeast wind blowing on the starboard side as they steamed southwest toward Cape Breton, but that wasn't strong enough to keep the 65-foot dragger listing.

After confirming that the crew were all together in the galley, Bob asked Walter to see if there was water on deck. When Walter confirmed the deck was partly awash, Bob knew for certain that something was definitely wrong. Alerting the crew members that the vessel was listing to port, Bob asked them to shift the trawl to the starboard side to try and balance the vessel. While the crew worked on the trawl, Bob called the *Zion* and *Cape York* to inform them that he might have trouble and asked if they would standby.

When Bob put the engine in gear again, the dragger quickly listed out to her port side.

"We got a big problem here," Bob said to Walter. "She must have developed a crack in the hull and water is getting in behind the steel plate and into the insulation."

Going down to the galley to tell the crew to get out their survival suits, Bob glanced out the galley door and noticed that the *Musn't Tell* had suddenly listed severely to port and was not righting. To make matters worse, it was now obvious that the vessel was going down by the stern. Without hesitation he shouted to the five crewmen to get to the life raft immediately as he ran to the wheelhouse to call the two nearby ships.

"We got a big problem," he shouted into the microphone. "I don't know what it is but please come alongside!"

Killing the engine power reduced the list somewhat but the dragger was rapidly going down at the stern. Two minutes later, the *Musn't Tell* was almost entirely under water.

Somehow, the five crew members made it into the life raft although it was still tied to the vessel.

"They were hollerin' at me to jump, but I was mostly underwater by then and still clinging to the boat and yelling back at them to cut the line to the life raft. The fella who was cooking that night had a little white paring knife for peeling potatoes with him and he managed to cut the line, setting the five of them free," Bob says.

When the port side of *Musn't Tell* sank level with the surface, Bob climbed up on the breakdeck by the wheelhouse to get a better view of what was going on. He could hear his 22-year-old son Bradley and the other four men in the life raft not far from the boat.

"I hollered to them to get the hell away because I was afraid the stabilizers on the boat would strike their life raft and throw them overboard." The starboard stabilizer was pointing straight up as the boat was listed 90 degrees to port. It was then that Bob started to swim away from his vessel but, as bad luck should have it, he wound up tangled in the twine that was half-submerged and half-floating off the deck of the vessel.

"I swam right into the f'n net, I did, and got tangled up in it underwater."

But, being tangled in twine didn't mean it was all over for Bob yet.

Luckily, the vessel's lights were still shining below the surface and Bob saw a piece of wood and managed to grab it. The buoyancy of the wood helped get him back to the surface, where he managed to untangle himself from the net and swim away from the stern of the vessel.

As Bob Truckair struggled to keep his head above water, he saw a frozen turkey that had floated up from the galley. "Everywhere I floated, that damn turkey kept moving in the same direction – like it was following me or something," he laughs.

Noticing that the seas and winds had swept the life raft from his view, Bob was succumbing to the freezing waters. As hypothermia advanced, Bob grew numb, but he remembers floating alongside the turkey once more and looking up at the wheelhouse of the *Musn't*

Tell, as it swayed back and forth in the wind and swell. The antennas on top of the wheelhouse would whip the water each time the superstructure went down, and although he was fighting for his life, Bob says he has vivid memories of everything at that point.

"I remember looking up at those aerials as they used to slash down alongside me. I said to myself, 'This is a queer f'n way that I'm gonna die tonight – me and that bloody turkey are gonna get carved up together.'"

To add to his woes, Bob saw two propane tanks shoot up from beneath the surface narrowly missing him.

"That's all I need now," he remembers thinking. "There were eight 100-pound tanks of them down there and they were shooting up like friggin' torpedoes. 'Supposing one of them hits me in the private parts,' I thought – I'd be finished then for sure."

Bob didn't get torpedoed by propane tanks, his private parts were still intact and he wasn't finished, although he wasn't far from giving up. Long past the point where most people would have become unconscious, Bob remained alert – at least alert enough to recognize that someone was calling to him. "It took awhile but I eventually realized that the Newfoundland boat was behind me and they had a light shining on me. I saw a young fellow climbing down over the side on a Jacob's ladder (rope ladder), while the skipper tried to manoeuvre the ship to get alongside." Bob called to the young man on the ladder, telling him that he was nearly frozen and too stiff to move. Once, Bob came close enough to the *Zion* that the man managed to grab him but couldn't hold fast long enough to pull him alongside.

"I got a rope," the man called, "I have to get this rope to you."

"Throw it," Bob called back. "Throw it around my neck if you have to. I'm going (to die) anyway. Just throw it!"

Clinging to the ladder with one hand, while trying to remain balanced as the ship rolled in the seas, the *Zion* crewman performed what would be the first of a series of miracles that saved Bob Truckair from dying that night. Somehow the crewman managed to get the rope around Bob's shoulders, giving him a solid grasp and keeping Bob close enough to work with. Climbing up the ladder a few feet, he threw the rope to other crew members on deck. They pulled Bob up the side of the large steel ship to safety.

"All I remember at that point was lying on the deck and the spotlights shining in my face and then everything went black. But Mister, I'm here to tell you that them guys, especially that young fella, did some job that night," Bob says gratefully.

After spending almost 45 minutes in the icy waters of the northwest Atlantic in December, Bob was suffering badly from hypothermia.

"When they started to thaw me out, they had to stuff something in my mouth because they were afraid my teeth were chattering so much that I'd bite my tongue off." The worst part of what Bob describes as "thawing out" was the pain in his hands.

"I thought they were going to explode – they felt like they were on fire," he says.

Bob's hands didn't explode and he didn't bite off his tongue.

After arriving in North Sydney late that night, Bob was examined by a doctor and released from hospital within hours. Bradley

Truckair and the other crewmen were rescued from the life raft and were all safely on board the *Cape York*.

After narrowly escaping what was perilously close to his *final voyage*, on December 2, 1989, Bob Truckair was merely sidelined for a brief period.

Three days later, Bob had leased another vessel and went back fishing again.

A Final Voyage for an Entire Community

Tony Sansome was just a young boy when he knew that he would be a fisherman when he grew up. Even before he was 10, Tony grabbed every opportunity he could find to go fishing with his father and uncle, even if it meant getting up at the crack of dawn. His mother, Thelma, remembers that Tony was so small when he insisted on going fishing with his dad, that the smallest rubber clothes she could find was much too big for her young son. "I had to cut the pant legs off to make them fit him," she says with a smile. When Tony graduated from high school in 1989 he wrote in the class yearbook that his "most probable fate" would be fishing from his homeport of Hillgrade, near Twillingate, in Notre Dame Bay. Within months, Tony Sansome fulfilled his high school prediction when DFO granted him a part-time fishing licence.

A quiet, mild-mannered young man, Tony was very serious about succeeding in his chosen profession.

"It takes a special breed to be a fisherman – you either got it or you don't, and Tony had it; he had what it takes to make it," says veteran Hillgrade fisherman Ches Coish. Ches lived next door to the Sansomes and watched Tony grow up, carefully monitoring his progress, helping and encouraging the young fisherman whenever he could. He was doing everything right according to Ches.

"He stayed at it, and he kept adding on a little more gear and a little more equipment and got newer and bigger boats – those sorts of things – and eventually he was going a little farther afield and doing good at it," Ches explains.

Tony Sansome was trying to build a fishing career in very difficult times. He acquired his full-time fishing licence just one year before the cod moratorium was imposed in 1992. Although he was swept up in the massive upheaval of fallout from that event, Tony somehow managed to achieve "core" status, something he really needed if he was going to continue fishing indefinitely. Despite a mountain of odds stacked against him, the young fishing skipper hung on and calculated his next moves strategically.

"Tony was careful in every way, and never took any unnecessary chances – he had a lot of common sense and could look ahead down the road and see how things were going to go," Ches Coish says.

Tony's mother, Thelma, agrees with Ches's assessment of her son. Thelma says Tony loved to read everything he could get his hands on that was written about the fishery; it was part of his way of learning more about his craft. One of his favourite sources of information was *The Navigator*.

"I was getting him a subscription to *The Navigator* for Christmas 2000," she says.

Older fishermen in Hillgrade took a special interest in Tony Sansome because, in many ways, he was the only hope they had in keeping the inshore fishery alive in their town. In the early 1990s, most would-be-fishermen in that area gave up on their dreams when the northern cod stock collapsed. Practically all the fishermen in Hillgrade were approaching retirement age and Tony's 35-foot boat would soon be the only small vessel heading out from the harbour each morning.

Like most fishermen, Tony Sansome loved sports and the outdoors. Also, like most fishermen, he was a hunter. During the first week of December in 2000, Tony and a friend embarked on a successful moose-hunting trip. On Thursday evening, December 7, 2000, Tony went to his fiancée, Sandra's home in nearby Summerford. While he waited for Sandra to get home from work, Tony phoned his mother saying that he was a little bored and laughed that when he got bored, he also got hungry. After making small talk with his mom about how to cook moose sausage, Tony hung up the phone and headed for the kitchen.

Sandra's young son was not feeling well that Thursday night, so Tony stayed over to be with them in case she needed a hand with anything. Sandra slept in the room with her child while Tony went to sleep in an adjoining room. At approximately six-thirty on Friday morning Sandra woke to the sound of what she first thought was Tony snoring loudly. Becoming more fully awake she suddenly realized that Tony was not snoring. Instead, she realized that was Tony making strange gasping sounds that didn't sound normal. Frightened, she rushed to the bedroom and, after taking a quick look at Tony, she hurried to the phone and called her brother next door to come quick because Tony was in some kind of trouble.

As a fireman, Sandra's brother knew how to administer CPR and started working on Tony while his sister called an ambulance. Sandra then called Tony's mother, Thelma, who immediately rushed to the Twillingate hospital. Minutes before she arrived, the ambulance attendants had brought her son to the emergency department, but it was too late.

Tony had already died.

No one knows for sure what happened to end Tony Sansome's life that morning. Even with an autopsy analysis, doctors are still mystified. Some have described it loosely as a kind of adult equivalent to what is commonly known as "crib death," where a person simply stops breathing. The only thing for certain is that Edward and Thelma Sansome lost their only child at age 29 on December 8, 2000.

Trying to cope with such a tragic loss has not been easy for the Sansome family, and Tony's unusual death has also dealt the small close-knit fishing community a painful blow. Because he was a gentle young man, it is fitting that Tony's family has donated a memorial hockey trophy in his name for the most gentlemanly and effective player in the minor hockey system in the New World Island and Twillingate region.

Unlike many fishermen, Tony's *final voyage* didn't occur at sea, but as Ches Coish is careful to point out, his death is more like a *final voyage* for the whole fishing community of Hillgrade.

"Without Tony Sansome to carry on behind us older fellows, an entire era may have made its *final voyage* with him."

The Other Man

Wednesday, June 2, 1982, was the day 56-year-old Lester Cull has been waiting for. Icebergs that had prevented Lester and his fishing partner Leander Ellsworth from setting their fishing nets all spring had finally moved offshore. The two long-time friends managed to set a few nets on Tuesday and as the sun rose over their homes in Englee on Wednesday morning, they knew this was the day they would start their fishing season.

There was no hurry. There had not been any sign of fish near Englee so far that spring, so it was unlikely the nets were full. Still though, by mid-morning, the sight of Lester's shiny new Mercury outboard motor sitting on the stern of his freshly painted 18-foot speedboat was hard to resist.

Shortly after 10:00 A.M., Leander and Lester, along with Lester's son Morris arrived in Barbour's Cove where the nets were set. Surprised at the good catch of codfish, the fishermen quickly set more nets before heading back home.

Tuning in to CBC Radio's *Fishermen's Broadcast* at five-thirty on Wednesday evening, Lester Cull was disappointed to hear that gale-force winds were forecast for Thursday. Wanting desperately to go fishing the next morning, he remembered the words of Uncle John Newman who always said, "you'd starve to death on the forecast my son." Smiling at Uncle John's wry sense of humour, Lester got his things together in case the forecast turned out to be wrong.

Uncle John Newman aside, the forecast was right on the mark. Leander and Lester both rose early Thursday morning to gale-force southeast winds accompanied by rain, drizzle and fog. On top of the foul weather, seas were running between seven and nine feet high. Disappointed, but pragmatic, both men knew that they wouldn't get out fishing until conditions improved.

Surprisingly, the weather improved much more quickly than expected. Shortly after 10:00 A.M., an impatient Lester phoned his friend.

"Leander," he said, "the wind has dropped. What do you say about going out?" It took awhile but Leander finally agreed that conditions might have improved enough to give it a try.

Less than an hour later, the two fishermen were passing Round Head just outside Englee Harbour on the way to check the first net. Despite seas that still ran high after the storm, Leander managed to hook the net float with the gaff while Lester manipulated the engine to steady the boat.

A minute later they saw the first glimpse of codfish rising through the dark blue water column. Concern about rough seas vanished as excitement and enthusiasm gave the men a surge of strength they thought was lost to their youth.

"Boy, does that ever look good," Leander exclaimed, talking more to himself than to Lester. At 57, Leander Ellsworth had caught his fair share of fish, but the season's first was as thrilling as ever.

After hauling the first fleet of gill nets, the two companions estimated they had 700 pounds of cod.

"And, I bet the other nets got just as many," Lester beamed.

He was right.

When Francis Compton and his crew steamed by about six o'clock that evening, Leander and Lester proudly showed off a fine catch of codfish. During a little lighthearted banter with his friends, Francis noticed that some of the highest waves had started to wash over the stern of his friend's boat.

"Lester, I think you have enough fish on board already," Francis said.

"Go on Francis, you're just jealous because we have more fish than you do," Lester laughed.

Although he was smiling at Lester's glee, Francis persisted. "Les," he continued, "if you're going to finish that fleet, you're going to have more than 2,000 pounds in that boat; let me take some in for you."

"Nah, that's alright boy, we'll be fine," replied Lester. "We'll be back in an hour or so." After unsuccessfully trying to convince Lester that he had too much fish on board already, Francis left and started the one-mile trip home to Englee.

When Francis arrived in Englee at approximately 6:30 P.M., Lester's wife, Maude, was becoming deeply concerned. A chronic worrier, she felt especially troubled that evening.

Tired of doing nothing but worry, Maude phoned Wilson Canning at the fish plant to inquire if anyone had seen her husband. Looking out his office window, Wilson saw Maude's son Morris along with his fishing partner Wilbert Randell putting away their day's catch of fish.

"I'll go down on the wharf right away and tell Morris," Wilson said.

"I know Mom worries too much, but as soon as we're finished we'll run out and take a look," Morris told Wilson.

Sadly, just minutes before his son was preparing to leave the harbour, Lester realized his boat was rapidly filling with water. Scrambling to keep the small speedboat afloat, Leander rushed forward to the bow, attempting to distribute the weight more evenly. At the same time, Lester started the engine in hopes of flushing some of the water back over the stern.

"If I can just get the boat moving fast enough," he sang out to Leander.

Fixated totally on watching the water action in the stern, neither man saw the big wave that was about to come crashing over them. Before they knew what happened, Leander was washed overboard.

As the engine sputtered and choked under the salt water, Lester grabbed the side of the boat and held on for dear life. Leander somehow managed to grab the painter (the line used for tying the boat to the wharf) and pulled himself back to the side of the partially swamped vessel. Considering their options, the two men realized there was nothing they could do but hang on and hope and pray that someone would come along soon.

At 6:45 P.M. Morris and Wilbert pushed their boat away from the wharf. Because Morris had been with his father when they set their nets on Wednesday, he knew exactly where to go, or so he thought. Not realizing the two overdue fishermen had set additional nets that afternoon, Morris was looking in the wrong spot.

Ironically, as Morris searched the waters, his father and Leander were just six or seven hundred feet away, still clinging on to the boat. But, the swamped boat was too low beneath the waves to see, and the noise of the engine combined with the wind and seas muffled calls for help.

As word of the missing men spread around the community, boats of all shapes and sizes searched the waters off Englee that night, but darkness and high waves prevented any sighting of the missing speedboat. At 2:00 A.M., several skippers considered the best thing to do was to wait until dawn. Worried that the small speedboat might be almost totally submerged, they were afraid of running over the men and doing more damage than good.

As dawn broke at four o'clock, Lester Cull's eldest son, Freeman, was on his way to the wharf to join veteran fishing captain

Cecil Randell on board the longliner *Alwyn Todd*. At approximately 4:30 A.M., just as the 40-foot longliner cleared Barr'd Island, slightly outside the mouth of Englee Harbour, crewman Wayne Randell sang out that he saw something.

"It's straight out there," he said, pointing his index finger in a due-south direction.

Freeman climbed upon the cabin of the fishing vessel, but shouted that he couldn't see anything.

"Maybe it's just a piece of ice then," Wayne said, still pointing his finger at what he thought was a floating object. "But then again, it's too dark to be ice," he mumbled.

Finally, Freeman spotted the object in his binoculars. Saying he first thought it was a whale, his voice suddenly turned excited.

"It's a boat, yes, yes boys, yes I can see a boat!" For a moment, Freeman was filled with joy. He thought he could see two men sitting in the flooded speedboat, but his excitement soon turned to disappointment. What at first looked like people sitting turned out to be the net-hauler in front and the engine on the stern.

In the wheelhouse, Cecil Randell pulled the *Alwyn Todd's* transmission level into neutral. As the longliner pulled near the half-submerged speedboat, Freeman, still standing on the wheelhouse, shouted, "There's Dad! There's Dad! That's Dad!"

Although his lifeless father's body was leaning to one side, he was in a sitting position with both eyes open, as if watching the rescuers approach. For a few moments Freeman was sure his father was alive but it soon dawned on him that his father was dead. As Freeman silently stared at the lifeless form of his father, Cecil hooked a gaff in the painter of the small boat.

"There's something on this painter," he said, pulling harder. Peering into the ocean as he tugged on the rope, Cecil soon realized he was pulling in the body of Leander Ellsworth.

Lester Cull had had an eerie premonition about his own *final voyage*. Several weeks before the accident, he dreamed that he saw two caskets. In one, was his friend Leander Ellsworth. As he told several people, including the pastor of his church in Englee, about the dream, Lester said he couldn't tell who the other person was.

In 1990, his son Freeman wrote a book about the tragedy. He titled it *Am I the Other Man?*

A Boat That Wouldn't Sink

Some boats sink within seconds.

Some boats just won't sink – no matter what.

While there are dozens of stories about vessels that went to the bottom within minutes, others seem to stay afloat against all odds. The 25-year-old longliner *Wavey Dale II* is still fishing, despite spending a day with her starboard side totally submerged after being pulled under by, among other things, a purse seine full of mackerel and herring.

Wes Caravan, owner of the 52-foot longliner, had been experiencing engine problems in the spring and summer fishery of 1985, so he installed a new Volvo 220-horsepower motor. When the installation was completed, it was time to go fishing herring and mackerel.

Monday morning, September 30, appeared to be an excellent morning for purse seining. Winds were westerly at about 15 knots and seas were calm, although there was a heavy tide running near Beaumont. Wes and his four crew members headed out that morning with the 160-fathom purse seine ready for action. About a mile offshore from Beaumont, they set their seine. Things went smoothly for a while. Wes estimated there were approximately 60,000 pounds of herring and mackerel in the seine when they started to winch it on board. The experienced crew worked steadily as they had done dozens of times before, removing the catch from the seine and stowing it below deck. When they had about half the seine emptied, Wes noticed the *Wavey Dale II* was listing to the starboard more than he thought was normal, considering the relatively small amount of fish on board.

Although he was not particularly worried about anything, Wes thought it would be a good idea to check below deck to make sure everything was OK. A quick inspection of the engine room showed no indication of trouble so he checked the hold. One quick look explained what had happened. Boards in the aft bulkhead had broken, and the 30,000 pounds of mackerel and herring had all shifted to the starboard side. As Wes started back to the deck, the *Wavey*

Dale II suddenly listed farther to starboard as if pulled down by some giant hand reaching up from the ocean. By the time Wes climbed on deck, the whole starboard side of his vessel was level with the ocean.

"When I looked around, the first thing I noticed was that the four crewmen had taken to the speedboat. Then I saw the keel of the boat two or three feet out of the water, so that's where I went – the only level part of the boat that was above water." A couple of minutes later, Wes was safe on board the speedboat with the other four men. Amazingly, no one was hurt, although one crewman had a close call. When the vessel tipped, Gus Rideout was standing between the boat's railing and the seine that was piled on deck. Somehow, he managed to scramble forward out of harm's way, when the net started sliding toward him. Had he become tangled in the net, Gus would have been in dire straits as the hundreds of feet of twine and ropes slid from the deck and sank beneath the surface.

After checking to make sure no one was hurt, Wes reviewed his options. The boat had tipped 90 degrees and was lying horizontally in the water, but the vessel didn't appear to be sinking any further. The stern section was more than half submerged because of the weight of the fish in the hold. Because the stern was mostly below water, the wheelhouse, located in the forward section of the vessel, was mostly above the surface. Realizing the vessel could start sinking at any moment, Wes decided to try and salvage a few things from the wheelhouse. Climbing up over the port bow, he eased himself down to the wheelhouse door.

"The only thing I managed to get out was the VHF Radio, but I saw something that made me laugh," he says. When water flooded in the submerged corner of the wheelhouse, several dozen mackerel flowed in with it. Given the circumstances, the sight was surreal according to Wes.

"All the mackerel were butting up against the windows of the wheelhouse trying to get out and here I was on the outside in the ocean, looking in and trying to get in where they were. It all seemed kind of strange," he laughs.

Giving up on the notion of trying to salvage anything from the wheelhouse, Wes and the crew turned their attention to saving the vessel from sinking. He had plenty of help. There were several other longliners fishing nearby who stopped fishing and came to provide whatever help they could. One of the skippers, Alwin Roberts from Robert's Arm, hooked a line to the *Wavey Dale II* and a few minutes later, the half-submerged vessel was under tow, limping to home port in Beaumont.

Not one to give up easily, Wes Caravan was determined to save the boat he built himself in 1974.

"We got a 'dozer and got her upright and then the fire department came and pumped her out," he says. Salt water damaged the electrics and the 12-year-old lube that stuck to the ceiling like cement was tough to deal with, but the *Wavey Dale II* was back fishing again in the spring of 1986.

Although he is sure it was more than the fish shifting in the hold, Wes is still not certain what caused the quick capsizing.

"I figure the tide ran between the boat and the seine in the water," he says. Possibly the tide pushed the seine away from the vessel putting more than the average strain on the cables causing it to tip all the way. Whatever the reason for the close call, one thing is certain, neither Wes Caravan nor the *Wavey Dale II* were ready for their *final voyage*.

Ghostly Message from a Drowning Brother

Roland Parsons loved fishing.

Although the John's Beach native worked at other jobs to support his family, he always held commercial fishing licences with the intention that as soon as it became economically viable, he would become a full-time fisherman. When the youngest of his children finished school, Roland told his wife, Jean, that the time had come for him to follow his dream. With Jean's support, Roland cut all ties with past employment and upgraded his fishing enterprise.

Like most of his inshore fishermen colleagues in the Bay of Islands, Roland's mainstay was the lobster fishery. To maximize the benefits of that fishery, Roland set up a small cabin on Big Island, about 20 kilometres away from John's Beach. With a roof over his head, a bunk to sleep in, and a stove to cook on and keep him warm,

Roland could stay on the island for several consecutive days instead of wasting time and money steaming from John's Beach to and from the fishing grounds every day. During the lobster season, he usually went to Big Island on Sunday evening and returned home on Friday evening for the weekend. Sometimes, his wife Jean went to the island with her husband.

The lobster fishery on Newfoundland's west coast was unusual in 1994. Heavy ice conditions in the Gulf of St. Lawrence delayed the opening date by nearly a month and nothing seemed to be normal until about the middle of June.

Roland Parsons's brother Howard was troubled about more than ice conditions that spring. Howard had experienced several recurring dreams where he saw an image of Roland lying in a casket. At first he dismissed the dreams as "foolishness" but when the same dream occurred again one night in late May, he decided that he should tell Roland about it. On Sunday, June 2, Howard visited his 56-year-old brother who was busy doing measurements and making other preparations to build a deck on the back of his house. As the men worked, Howard thought that this would be a good time to tell his brother about his strange dreams.

"I wanted to tell him to be extra careful on the water," Howard says.

Howard never did tell his brother about his concerns. A family friend dropped by and chatted as the two men worked on the deck. Howard felt that his dream was an awkward subject to broach in mixed company. After they finished working, Howard went home while Roland and Jean gathered their supplies and prepared to leave later that evening for Big Island for another week.

The trip to Big Island was uneventful for Roland and his wife. The next day, Monday, June 3, was unusually cool but otherwise an ordinary day, at least until Monday night. When Roland woke up early Tuesday morning, he was amazed to see that about six inches of snow had fallen overnight. Other than having to deal with snow and unseasonably low temperatures, there was no other reason to stay ashore that morning. Winds were moderate but not expected to increase. After chatting with fellow fishermen Max Strickland, George Wheeler and Gerald Strickland, Roland boarded his dory at 6:25 A.M. and headed out from the cove to start checking his lobster traps. About 15 or 20 minutes later, Roland's friends left their moorings and headed out on the water too. After a five-minute steam, the Stricklands and George Wheeler saw Roland Parsons's dory speeding around and around in circles. There was no sign of Roland.

Unable to get close enough to the runaway speedboat to determine whether Roland might have suffered a heart attack or something and was perhaps lying on the floor of the boat, the fishermen could only wait until the engine ran out of gas or the dory went ashore. With each circle, the dory was getting nearer and nearer to land and finally grounded near the beach. When there was no sign of Roland in or near the dory, the fishermen did a quick scan of the shoreline and the ocean, but choppy seas made it impossible to get a good view. They decided the most prudent thing to do under the circumstances was to go back to their cabin and contact the RCMP in Corner Brook.

At 7:45 A.M. Howard Parsons received a phone call saying his brother was missing.

"When did he leave the beach?" Howard asked. When the caller answered "Six-twenty-five," Howard nodded. "Yes, and he went overboard at six-thirty," he replied, knowingly.

Today, Howard explains why he responded that way. At six-thirty that morning Howard says he bolted upright in bed from a sound sleep.

"I remember I was gasping for breath and feeling panicky and my arms were waving, like I was trying to tread water or something. Somehow, I think Roland sent me a message," he says.

Meanwhile, Roland's youngest brother, Roger Parsons, also received a phone call that morning. A fisherman like his older brother and living in John's Beach, Roger knew the waters around Big Island very well and immediately started to get ready to go and search.

"I'm coming with you," his wife Maureen said, wanting to be with her husband in case something had gone wrong. By approximately 8:30 A.M., Roger and Maureen were steaming into a fairly stiff northwesterly breeze coming directly into the Bay of Islands. Just as they neared Big Island, Maureen shouted over the roar of the outboard motor to her husband, saying that they had just passed something floating in the water. Roger hadn't seen anything, but decided to circle back and take a look anyway. Moments later, Roger Parsons was horrified to recognize his brother floating face down and lifeless in the water.

It was difficult, but Roger and Maureen somehow managed to pull Roland from the sea and into the dory. Although the fishing cabins on Big Island were just a few minutes away, Roger did not want to go there. Trying to come to grips with his own emotions, Roger couldn't comprehend how to tell Jean that Roland was dead. That's when fate made the decision for Roger. Just as they were abeam of Roland's stranded dory on the shoreline, the engine suddenly shut off.

"No matter what I tried, I couldn't get that engine started, yet there was nothing obvious wrong with it. It was just like we couldn't get past Roland's boat for some reason. It was almost ghostly like," Roger says, still mystified by the eerie moment. As he frantically tried to start the outboard motor, a RCMP helicopter appeared overhead. Using hand signals to communicate with the crew in the chopper, Roger was able to explain that he had retrieved his brother's body.

Minutes later, Gerald Strickland arrived on the scene and started towing them to shore where the helicopter had landed. Incredibly, once under tow, Roger's outboard motor started easily.

As with most tragedies when there is no one left to tell the story, we will never know exactly what happened that morning. Howard Parsons said he personally checked the body to see whether the engine's propeller had hit Roland when he fell overboard. There was no sign that Roland had suffered an injury. Howard feels his brother, who usually stood up while steering the speedboat, slipped on snow or ice and fell overboard. Although Roland could swim, the icy cold waters in the Bay of Islands that spring would have caused the hypothermic process to start within 10 or 12 minutes.

Sadly, like many similar cases, the only thing certain is that Roland Parsons made his *final voyage* on June 4, 1994.

A Dream Like No Other

Fred Wall was just a young boy when he decided that he was going to be a fisherman like his dad. Like many boys from Campbellton, he couldn't wait for the times when his father, Alfred Wall, would ask if Fred wanted to join him in the fishing boat the next day. Later, when Fred had sons of his own, he continued the family tradition.

When the lobster season opened in Notre Dame Bay, Newfoundland, in May 1964, Fred's 16-year-old son, Clarence, already a seasoned fisherman, was happy to give his dad a hand at setting the lobster traps. The first couple of days of the season produced good landings, so the father and son team decided to put out additional traps. After setting approximately 20 lobster pots in the morning, Fred and Clarence returned home for lunch in the early afternoon.

Seeing Fred's small 17-foot boat tied up at the wharf, Ambrose Wall dropped by his brother's house to get an update on the lobster news from that morning. Ambrose didn't stay long. He had a truck-load of lobsters to take to Lewisporte for shipment. Before Ambrose left to make the 10-mile trip, the two brothers discussed the weather, wondering if it would be okay for Fred and young Clarence to set out a few more pots before suppertime. Both men agreed the weather appeared fine and there shouldn't be anything to worry about. As Ambrose was leaving his brother's house heading for his truck, Fred said he figured he would set the lobster traps around Mickey Island.

"We'll probably stay out overnight on the island," he told his brother. Fred shared a summer fishing camp with Hedley Cramm on the small island about six miles out of the bay from Campbellton. Darkness would be creeping in by the time he and Clarence finished setting the pots, and the 37-year-old fishermen was concerned about the large number of ice pans in the bay that spring.

Ambrose didn't worry about his brother and nephew until he was nearly in Lewisporte. The wind suddenly chopped around from the northeast and whitecaps had already developed on the bay.

"Looking across the bay there, I wondered if Fred had his traps all set and had made it to the island before the wind changed," Ambrose remembers thinking.

Ambrose finished his business in Lewisporte and was driving back home just as darkness was falling. The wind was still northeast-erly and by then a heavy fog blanketed the Notre Dame Bay coastline. As Ambrose drove along the winding dirt road towards Campbellton, the driver of a car coming in the opposite direction flagged him down. Recognizing the driver as Pastor Roy Kearley, Ambrose knew that something was wrong. His instinct was well-founded. Pastor Kearley said that several lobster traps had washed up on the shoreline in Campbellton late in the afternoon and some fishermen wondered if they belonged to Fred. Ambrose knew that his brother and Clarence were the only fishermen in the community setting pots that day, so the pastor and the others were right to be concerned.

With visibility reduced to almost nil in the thick fog, Ambrose knew it would be dangerous picking his way through the ice-infested waters, but he also knew he had to find out if Fred and Clarence were safe in their cabin on Mickey Island. Without a compass on board his small open boat, Ambrose judged his direction by the winds and seas until he could see the outline of island's cliffs, a few feet in front of his boat.

On the island, Hedley Cramm was listening for any sound of approaching boats; he was afraid that his buddy Fred was having trouble finding the island in the thick fog. When Ambrose pulled in by the small wharf, Hedley was waiting.

"Are Fred and Clarence in there?" Ambrose called from the boat.

When Hedley said he hadn't seen his fishing partner since morning, Ambrose didn't even shut off his engine. Heading back toward Campbellton as fast as he dared in the thick fog, it was just by chance that he didn't strike the overturned and submerged hull of his brother's boat, just 50 feet from the shoreline of Woody Duck Island, about a mile away from Campbellton.

Hoping that Fred and Clarence had made it ashore somewhere, Ambrose hurried home to organize a search party.

Search crews didn't spend much time looking for bodies near Woody Duck Island, because they knew that was not where the two lobster fishermen were setting their traps. Everyone agreed that the small boat was likely capsized by a wave near Mickey Island, several miles away. The boat quickly drifted toward Woody Duck Island, coming to rest only when the grapnel, hanging down from the bow of the boat, snagged on the bottom in shallow water. For five long days, fishermen, police officers and anyone who wanted to help, scraped the ocean floor with jiggers and other types of hooks hoping to find the bodies. Concentrating their efforts in the vicinity where they were certain the boat capsized, boat after boat cautiously criss-crossed the bay but found nothing.

On the morning of day six, just as several boats were preparing to continue the search, 14-year-old Willis Wall approached one of the men and quietly stated that he knew where the bodies were located. He had a dream, he said. But it was too real to be just an ordinary dream. In his dream he clearly saw the bodies of his father and brother lying on the bottom.

Not wanting to dismiss any possibility, the men helped the youth on board a search boat as Willis directed the skipper to go to where the victim's boat was found six days earlier. "That's where they are," he said. "They're on the bottom, where the boat was found." Within minutes, Willis and the search team were about 40 feet offshore from the beach of Woody Duck Island silently staring down through four feet of water at the bodies of the missing fishermen.

No one knows exactly what happened to Fred and Clarence of course, but Ambrose Wall believes that his brother and nephew managed to climb onto the bottom of the overturned speedboat where they intended to hang on until their boat ceased to drift. But then the grapnel struck bottom. Without life jackets – and perhaps by then in an advanced state of hypothermia after two or three hours in the freezing water – neither of the two could make it to safety onto the island. Sadly, the beginning of the 1964 lobster season marked the *final voyage* of Fred and Clarence Wall.

Close Encounter with a Sea "Monster"

"Look out, Peter!" yelled Felix and Eugene Jones to their brother.

Peter Jones never did see what his brothers tried to warn him about. A split-second after their yell, all three fishermen were thrown into the waters of Placentia Bay.

Wednesday, June 10, 1992 had started out as most other days for the Jones brothers. The morning broke foggy with a light easterly wind blowing into the mouth of Baine Harbour on the Burin Peninsula. As day dawned, the hum of diesel engines and outboard motors echoed across the harbour as a dozen or more fishing boats headed out to their Placentia Bay cod fishing grounds. Felix and

Eugene Jones sat in the front of their 21-foot speedboat straining to see if there were boats or any signs of danger in the thick fog. Back aft, 27-year-old Peter Jones, head of the fishing enterprise, kept a wary eye on the compass as he set a course for 12 miles to the southeast. About an hour later, Felix called for his brother's attention, pointing to a small red buoy, barely visible through the fog. All three men smiled quietly in anticipation of a good day fishing as they prepared to haul the first fleet of gill nets. Peter's navigational reckoning had been dead on through the fog – so far, so good.

Shortly after noon the fog lifted and the sun broke through the high cloud. The sun's warmth, combined with a reasonably good catch of 1,200 pounds of cod that morning boosted the spirits of the three fishermen. After a break for lunch, Felix and Eugene were situated in the boat's mid-section looking at Peter who was standing on the aft port side preparing to gut more fish. With the motor and the CB radio shut down, the only sounds came from waves lapping against the side of the fibreglass boat. Life seemed about as good as it gets.

Suddenly, the tranquility was violently shattered.

As Felix and Eugene watched in disbelief, a huge gray-black monster reared up from the ocean, lunging at the boat, directly toward Peter who was facing in the opposite direction. As the two brothers in the boat's mid-section screamed at Peter to "Look out!" the monster with a huge tooth-filled mouth came crashing down across the small plywood housing built on the starboard side of the boat. The boat and everything in it was flipped in the air and landed bottom up.

In shock, Peter Jones desperately tried to figure out what had just happened. Why was he suddenly in the ocean treading water? What happened to the boat? What was that huge dark gray mass that he saw briefly from the corner of his eye as he was thrown from the boat? Did he really see something or was all this just a horrible dream? Where were his brothers?

When the initial shock began to subside, Peter noticed the front of his overturned boat several feet away. Swimming towards the almost totally submerged vessel, Peter could hear Eugene shouting. Suddenly, he realized that both Eugene and Felix had surfaced underneath the overturned hull.

Although neither Eugene nor Felix could swim, they realized they that they had to get out from underneath the boat quickly. Steadying themselves by gripping whatever part of the boat they could grasp, both managed to control their fear of going under water again and soon surfaced several feet away from where Peter was anxiously waiting to see them. During the process of getting out from under the boat, 20-year-old Eugene realized that his brother Felix had suffered a blow to the head. More dazed than frightened, Felix was only partially aware of what was happening around him.

"Felix is going down," Eugene called to Peter. "You gotta help him."

Peter, the only swimmer among the three, grabbed his brother but soon both men started going down.

"He was like grabbing hold to an anchor," Peter recalls. Kicking off his heavy work boots, Peter held on to his brother and finally managed to get them both to the surface long enough to yell to Felix that he had to try and help keep himself afloat. Although he was barely aware of what was going on, Felix understood Peter's plea and started moving his arms enough to keep his head above water as Peter dragged him toward the boat.

With the weight of the heavy outboard motor pulling the aft section of the boat underwater, only four or five feet of the bow section was afloat. Peter crawled on the slippery hull first and then Eugene followed. Grabbing an arm each, Peter and Eugene then managed to drag Felix from the ocean and laid him face down across the keel.

Safe atop the speedboat, the brothers enjoyed a few moments of relative comfort. But a few moments was all it lasted. A wave soon washed against the boat and even though it was just a small lop, it caused the submerged motor to swing and then jerk the boat to one side. Before they could brace themselves, all three were thrown overboard again.

They didn't keep count of how many times they were washed overboard and had to crawl back on top again, but Peter says it went on all afternoon. Because the boat was extremely low in the water, Felix's feet, arms and legs were often in the water when the boat rolled. He was weak and unable to sit or stand. Lying astride the keel was his only option.

As if constantly being washed overboard wasn't enough misery to contend with, the men were keenly aware that they didn't get into this predicament because of rough seas, high winds or a collision with another boat. The "thing" that capsized their boat, known to them only as the "monster," still might come back. Several hundred dead fish that spilled from their boat still floated near them. If the monster was still close enough it might be attracted to the dead fish and come closer to investigate. Once, a couple of humpback whales surfaced nearby. Seeing

Peter Jones.

such a huge animal surfacing so near sent chills up and down their already almost-frozen spines.

Back in Baine Harbour, their father kept an eye on the clock as he watched several fishermen returning to port that afternoon. An experienced trawlerman, Tom Jones grew very worried when the last of the other boats arrived and there was still no sign of his sons.

"They should have been here about two hours ago," Tom said to his friend Melvin Murphy.

"I allow their engine broke down," Melvin replied.

"How about if we took a look around out there?" Tom asked his friend.

Melvin didn't need arm-twisting. Neither man said anything, but both were thinking about their friend Tom Keating, a Baine Harbour fisherman who had drowned just four weeks earlier.

Tom grew extremely anxious when they arrived at the location where his sons would have been fishing. It would soon be dark and searching for a small boat at night in Placentia Bay was akin to looking for a needle in a haystack.

"Let's check and see how the tide is running," Tom said to Melvin. Once they determined that the tide was running to the southeast, the two men headed in that direction, thinking that if the Jones brothers had engine problems their speedboat would have drifted that way.

Their knowledge of the sea paid off. With only minutes left before darkness fell, Tom saw something in the distance that gave him hope. A minute later he could see his son Peter standing on the nearly submerged hull of his speedboat.

An ambulance from the Burin hospital met the rescuers when they arrived home in Baine Harbour. Peter and Eugene didn't require medical attention but Felix was in bad shape. Late that night a doctor told the Jones family that Felix would be fine, but that in his weakened condition, another half an hour in the frigid water would almost surely have killed him.

Ten years later, the Jones brothers are still not sure what kind of monster attacked them that day. Judging from the teeth marks it left in the plywood, some marine experts think it must have been a great white shark. Although very uncommon to waters as far north as

Newfoundland, fishermen say there have been a few sightings of great whites in Placentia Bay. No other animal seems to fit the profile of the behavior exhibited by this creature and although Felix and Eugene only saw it for a few seconds, their descriptions also suggest a strong likeness to the most feared animal in the oceans.

Peter, Felix and Eugene Jones are not particularly fussy whether they ever find out what their "monster" was. The most important thing to them is that whatever it was, it didn't take them on their *final voyage.*

Seabird Hunting Trip Turns into Battle for Survival

Eli Martin survived a crash landing in a DC-3 once. The aircraft was a write-off, but the man from Grates Cove, known to everyone as Junior, walked away without a scratch. Spending two and a half hours in the bone-chilling frigid waters of the northwest Atlantic after falling through the ice during a sealing trip didn't bother him much either. But Junior got a bit worried once in 1973 when he and his fishing buddy, 22-year-old Dave Stanford, got caught in a winter blizzard just off the northwestern tip of the Avalon Peninsula.

The weather on Friday morning, January 5, 1973, was as good as it gets around Trinity Bay in winter. With bright sunshine and flat, calm waters, the two fishermen figured it was a great day to try out Junior's brand new 20-horsepower Mercury outboard motor. Junior hadn't even used a single tank of gas on the new motor he'd bought to go on his 16-foot boat. There hadn't been many turrs sighted so far that winter, and this would be a good day to check things out, they thought. Anxious to replenish the deep-freezer with their favourite seabird delicacy, Dave and Junior set out at 8:00 A.M. and steamed about five miles to Baccalieu Island, east of Grates Cove. To their delight, it wasn't long before they had about 25 turrs in the little flat-bottomed boat.

At approximately 10:00 A.M. a stiff southerly breeze sprang up quickly. With weather and sea conditions no longer appropriate for hunting, Eli turned the small boat to the west and headed for home. Suddenly, and for no obvious reason, the outboard motor stopped running. Junior, a 32-year-old experienced fisherman, didn't think much about it much at first; after all, the engine was brand new and surely it would be just a matter of pulling the cord and off they'd go again.

He was wrong.

Although Junior did everything he could, the motor would not start. With the winds and waves growing higher and higher, the two decided to try rowing towards land, but strong southerly winds battering the small boat from the broadside were too much for them to handle. In hopes of attracting the attention of someone onshore, Dave and Junior raised a jacket on an oar as a makeshift signal flag, but seas were too high and no one noticed them. Although they could still see their hometown only two miles away, the men needed to turn their attention to simply staying afloat rather than trying to make it to port. While seas continued to toss the little boat around like a cork, Junior used a sculling oar to keep the boat running before the wind to avoid capsizing.

As the gap between the boat and Grates Cove widened, things grew worse. The temperature fell below freezing and it started snowing. About 3:30 P.M. darkness closed in and, combined with the drifting snow, this meant Junior and Dave no longer had any idea which way they were heading. As the storm raged, the only thing left to do was lie down on the bottom of the small boat and hope for the best. Lying there was frightening.

"Looking up at those big dark 20-odd foot waves coming at ya, wondering if this was going to be the one, was not a very good feeling," Dave says.

Dave and Junior had no way of knowing at the time, but things would get a lot worse before they got better. At approximately 8:00 P.M., what appeared to be a huge black cloud loomed directly in front of them. Straining to see if it was a cloud, fog or land, Dave fired his shotgun. The light from the gun's flash illuminated the face of a steep black cliff towering about 300 feet above them.

Moments later, the small boat was smashed against a rock.

Both men scrambled to jump for safety. Dave, who was in the front of the boat, made it onto a rock, but the boat was split into pieces before Junior could jump. Dave, standing on an ice-covered rock the size of a kitchen table, couldn't see his friend anywhere.

For his part, Junior remembers washing in and out with the waves, underwater more often than he was on top.

"I could hear Dave yelling out to me when I'd come up, but I couldn't do anything but try to hang on for a few seconds before getting washed away again." Once, Junior surfaced near what appeared to be a large piece of the splintered boat. He grabbed it, but the board was tossed end over end by a wave and came crashing down against the side of his face, cracking off a tooth.

Miraculously, Junior, by then, dazed and battered, washed up against the rock where Dave was standing. Dave caught a glimpse of his partner and grabbed his coat. Although Junior was hardly able to help himself, Dave somehow managed to hold on until he pulled his friend safely on the rock with him. Together again, the two men found renewed strength to carry on.

Although they were safe for a few moments, it was obvious they had to get to land. Perched on an icy rock 200 feet offshore in a January storm was not a place they could survive the night. One big wave could carry them offshore to their doom in seconds. Although neither man could swim, they both jumped from the rock into the ocean and for the first time in many hours they were blessed with a stroke of luck. The water was only chest-high and they managed to claw their way through the slob ice and onto a small, rocky ledge at the base of the cliff.

But the longest night of their lives was just beginning. There was no beach, so even if there were driftwood and other materials to build a shelter from the storm, there was no place to put it. The only thing they could do was stand on the tiny ledge and wait until day-

(l-r) Dave Stanford, Eli Martin.

light. Soaked to the bone and bitterly cold, Junior and Dave knew they had to keep moving to stay alive.

"We jumped up and down and danced around all night on that little ledge," Junior remembers.

After what seemed like an eternity, the dark sky brightened as daylight eased up into the eastern sky. The snow stopped falling and the winds dropped but the temperature fell well below freezing.

"Our wet clothes froze as solid as a rock," Dave says. Weakened from the bone-chilling cold, the two were growing even more tired from hunger and the lack of sleep. More than 24 hours had passed since they last ate, but there was no time to worry about minor details like hunger, the need to rest or, in Junior's case, an injury. Determined to see his wife and young children again, the older of the two men was oblivious to his pain.

As soon as they could see, Dave and Junior started the long, steep climb to the top of the cliff. Luckily there was a tree that had broken and had grown out from the tip of the cliff.

"We managed to grab that tree and haul ourselves to the top. That's the only way we could have made it," Dave says. Despite waist-high snow and thick forests, the men trudged along, hoping to get a glimpse of something to give them a clue where they were.

"We didn't know the wind changed in the evening and we drifted in a different direction than we thought," Junior recalls.

"We knew we weren't near Grates Cove because there were too many trees," Dave laughs, referring to the barren landscape near their hometown.

After an incredibly long and arduous morning trudging slowly across bogs and marshes, both men were starting to become delirious. They were convinced they could see a cabin through the trees once but it turned out to be an illusion.

"We must have suffered some snow-blindness too, because we'd fall down but we were not able to see that we were falling," Dave says. "Each time one of us would fall, the other one would go back and give the other one a shake and a few words of encouragement to get up and go on," Junior says with a smile.

Finally, they saw a transmission pole in the distance. Knowing that there would probably be a road nearby, they found enough strength to make it to a hill where they could see what turned out to be the Bonavista Highway.

"As soon as the first vehicle came along, we jumped out in the middle of the road and started waving. There was no way he could get past us," Dave laughs.

Half an hour later, Junior and Dave were guests at the Prominent Spur Hotel in Port Union. A doctor came and examined them. Amazingly, after an experience that would have killed most people, both men were given a clean bill of health.

"Dave had a small frostbite and I couldn't swallow because I had taken a little too much saltwater, but other than that, we were fine," Junior says.

Despite their amazing survival against all odds, both Dave Stanford and Junior (Eli) Martin are well aware how close they came to making their *final voyage* on January 5 and 6, 1973.

Wife's Eerie Premonition
Almost Deadly Accurate

The boys are in trouble!

Those words kept echoing through Kathleen Dawe's mind as she practically leaped out of bed in the early morning hours of June 18, 1992.

The 60-year-old woman from Torbay still can't explain exactly what she felt when she suddenly awoke at five o'clock that Thursday morning, but she knew something had gone wrong. She also knew that it had to do with her husband Will, her two sons and a grandson, all fishing on the Grand Banks on the 47-foot longliner *Paula and Jordan*. Unable to get back to sleep, Kathleen went downstairs and made a cup of tea. Her daughter, Jeannie, who was in the kitchen getting ready for work, wondered why her mother was up so early. Before Jeannie could ask, Kathleen told her daughter about her strange sensation. "The boys are in trouble; I just know there is trouble on the boat," she said.

Kathleen Dawe's premonition was correct – almost deadly accurate.

The previous evening, Kathleen's son, 31-year-old Bill Dawe, the owner and skipper of the *Paula and Jordan*, decided to head for Fermuse, 120 miles away, to repair a broken gurdy (net hauler). All night, the longliner inched along in the strong winds and high seas, but just before dawn, about the same time that Kathleen felt an overwhelming sense of impending disaster, the winds had increased to near-gale force from the northeast and seas ran 30 feet high. When daylight broke, the *Paula and Jordan* was 60 miles east of Cape Race. That's when the crew noticed the longliner was taking on more water than the pumps could handle. When three of the vessel's seven pumps failed, Bill knew they were in big trouble. Struggling to keep his vessel "head-to" in the winds and seas, Bill issued a mayday. Other fishing vessels in the area heard the call and went to the scene, but the then 40-foot seas were too wild for them to approach the sinking longliner.

Meanwhile, the Coast Guard also heard the distress signal and dispatched a helicopter to the area.

"We were pretty happy to see that chopper," says Bill, "I don't think we could have held on much longer." Little did the young skipper know that he would have to hang on a lot longer – nearly eight hours longer, before he was lifted off his vessel.

At first, everyone wondered whether they could even get a line from the chopper to the boat as it tossed around on the seas. Things went reasonably well for a little while. Search and Rescue (SAR) technicians Bill Barber and Tom Taylor were carefully lowered from the chopper on a cable "hoist" and landed on the deck of the stricken vessel without a problem. The first man selected to go up was Will Dawe, the skipper's father. After putting the "horsecollar" on the 58-year-old fisherman, Barber signalled the chopper engineer to hoist both of them.

That's when things started to go wrong.

Just as the cable began to tighten, the *Paula and Jordan* lunged from the crest of a huge wave, sliding down 40 feet into the trough. When the helicopter pilot lost sight of the boat, he went higher to get a new visual reference while at the same time the boat was in a free-fall. At the end of the cable hoist, Bill Barber and Will Dawe were catapulted across the deck and slammed into five vertical metal railings at the stern of the vessel. At first, the cable stretched like an elastic band but then tightened and snapped, flipping the two men high into the air. Amazingly, they both landed directly between the same metal pipes that, just seconds before, had kept them from going overboard.

"If they had come down a few inches either side, they would have been skivered onto the pipes and a few inches farther back they would have landed in the water; either way they would have died," Bill Dawe says.

Although dazed and injured, SAR tech Bill Barber was in control of the operation again within minutes. Realizing the broken cable had taken away their only lifeline, Barber shouted at the pilot to radio for another chopper. At the same time, the flight engineer was frantically rigging up a second cable, one that drops from the centre of the aircraft. Because the centre cable on a Labrador helicopter is farther away from the cockpit, the pilot can't see what is going on below, making rescue attempts extremely difficult in rough seas. But with four fishermen and two of their own colleagues stranded on the deck of the boat, there was no choice. They had to get another line down.

Dropping smoke canisters into the ocean as markers for the pilot's reference, the engineer lowered the hoist until Barber was able to grab it. Moments later, Barber and Will Dawe were in the air again. This time they made it to the chopper. Undaunted by a brush with death just minutes before, Barber went down again, this time to get 19-year-old Jimmy Oakley.

Despite feeling good about their success so far, the SAR team soon faced a new dilemma. Airborne for hours, the chopper was nearly out of fuel. After hoisting Tom Taylor from the boat, there was no time left to get Bill and his 28-year-old brother Randy Dawe. The chopper had to get to Cape Race immediately. Shouting a promise to return, Bill Barber took another look at the two men on the deck of the sinking vessel. Sharing their feeling of helplessness, he too wondered how much longer the boat would stay afloat. With winds still increasing and 40-foot seas crashing over the sinking vessel, Bill and Randy were sure they would die.

"When I saw them leave, I thought they'd never get another chopper out in weather like that," Bill Dawe says.

About the same time the chopper landed in Cape Race, Bill Dawe's wife, Shelly, received a phone call from a friend saying that the *Paula and Jordan* was sinking. The friend said the chopper had returned from the scene with two of the crew, but she didn't know who they were.

"That's when I lost it," Shelly says. Racing to St. John's, Shelly went straight to the harbour and jumped on board a longliner owned by friends. Within an hour, about 20 other family members joined

*Bill Dawe hoisted from the **Paula & Jordan**.*

Shelly as they all listened intently to Marine Radio for updates on what was happening.

"It was the longest day of my life, especially the hours when there was no chopper on the scene," Shelly admits, shaking her head slowly. "It was the not knowing whether the boat was still afloat and whether there was even a chance of saving Bill and Randy. That was the worst."

At Cape Race, things took a turn for the better in the afternoon. As Bill Barber and his colleagues touched down with only a few gallons of fuel remaining in the tanks, the second helicopter arrived. Bill and Tom ran from their chopper to the other one and, within minutes, they were on the way out again. At times slowed almost to a standstill by gale-force winds, it took the chopper an hour to get to the *Paula and Jordan*. Relief swept over the rescuers when they saw the longliner floating with Bill and Randy still in reasonably good condition. Bill Barber was on deck again within minutes, first taking Randy and then Bill Dawe to safety in the waiting chopper. Just after Bill Dawe was secure on the helicopter, the *Paula and Jordan* rolled over and sank, as if waiting for the appropriate time.

Will Dawe retired from fishing following his rescue. Young Jimmy Oakley decided that fishing was not for him and pursued a career on dry land. Bill Dawe was on another boat headed back to sea two days later. However, the loss of the *Paula and Jordan* was not the last time the young fishing captain would narrowly escape his *final voyage*.

Gone in the Blink of an Eye

Like most fishing skippers, Bill Dawe was not prepared to give up fishing simply because he lost a vessel and he, along with his crew, narrowly escaped death. Soon after the sinking of the Paula and Jordan, *Bill was steaming out from St. John's Harbour in a new fishing vessel ready to face whatever challenges the sea could offer. Amazingly though, the ocean was not finished testing the courage and ability the young fishing captain and his crew from Torbay, Newfoundland.*

"Whatever happened, it happened awful quick – she was gone within a minute."

That's the way Bill Dawe describes the sinking of his 55-foot fishing vessel, *Morning Dove*, August 3, 1998.

Monday morning was a fine midsummer's day off Black Tickle, Labrador. The skipper and four-man crew of the *Morning Dove* had fished the area all weekend and were up before dawn on Monday, eager to start another full day of shrimp fishing in ideal weather conditions.

Shortly after daybreak, crewmen Ken Whiteway, Greg Reid and David Reid had shot away the net from the stern of the vessel, while the skipper was in the wheelhouse keeping tabs on engine speed and other control levers as they prepared to haul back their first tow. Derek Wells was in the galley, in the front of the vessel, preparing breakfast.

Within a few seconds after starting to "take back," Greg and David realized that something was wrong. The net was snagged in something. Following normal procedure, they towed from another direction hoping to free it. It didn't work. Finally, on the third try, it appeared the net had broken free and, for a while, things appeared to be going fine.

In the wheelhouse, Skipper Bill Dawe was talking on the sideband radio to Terry Bungay on board the longliner *Roberts Sisters*, fishing nearby. As he chatted with his friend, Bill was keeping a close eye on what was happening on deck.

"I was watching Greg getting ready to hook the net to start hoisting it on board when I heard someone yell, 'something is not right here!'"

In the galley, Derek must have heard the call or sensed that something was wrong. He ran up the stairs as quickly as he could and headed toward the deck.

Shouting into the radio microphone that he'd call Terry back, Bill started running behind Derek. He didn't make it through the door. Something was quickly pulling the *Morning Dove* under water stern first and water was plowing in over the fishing gear toward the wheelhouse.

Derek made it to the deck, and although Bill was just a couple of feet behind his friend, he was a few seconds too late. As water rushed through the wheelhouse door, Bill was swept backwards in the heavy flow and pinned against the steering wheel. With only a few seconds to make decisions, Bill knew that if he got swept into the galley, he'd never make it back through the water to safety outside. Desperately clinging to the wheel, the 37-year-old skipper remained surprisingly cool and rational. Suspecting the others had been washed overboard, he grabbed the gearshift and tried to put the still-running engine into neutral.

"At least, that way, the boys wouldn't get cut on the blade if they fell in that area," he remembers thinking.

Bill's well-intentioned manoeuvre might have placed himself in double jeopardy. Instead of pulling the shift lever to neutral, he thinks he might have pulled it too far, driving it into reverse position. The vessel started sinking even more quickly and within seconds, the *Morning Dove* had totally filled with water and rolled over. By the time the steel vessel settled, most of the keel and the propeller were above the surface but the skipper was trapped underwater inside the wheelhouse.

In the first of what some people might describe as a series of miracles, Bill managed to find a small pocket of air in the port corner of the wheelhouse, near the floor. Keeping his head above water, he managed to grab the floating radio microphone and yelled "Mayday!" Because the radio was nearly submerged in saltwater, Bill didn't know if his call was heard or not.

As Bill suspected, all four men on deck were washed overboard when the *Morning Dove* rolled over. Ken, Derek and Greg surfaced near the overturned vessel and managed to climb up on the overturned hull. David surfaced next to a wooden table that had washed from the deck. Although holding on to the table helped keep his head above water, David was rapidly losing body heat in the freezing cold water.

As the *Morning Dove* continued to fill with water, it rolled from side to side. Sometimes the after-tow carried the table and David close to the boat, but not near enough for the young man to get off the table and onto the bottom of the boat with his colleagues. On a couple of occasions, David even caught a glimpse of Bill through the wheelhouse window underwater. Seeing Bill trapped inside the vessel added to David's anxiety.

"Bill is dead, Bill is dead! I can see him in the wheelhouse," he yelled to the others. "I can see his eyes through the glass – he's dead."

Bill was not dead.

During the next "miracle," the boat rolled and heaved in such a way that the wheelhouse door was pushed open by the force of the sloshing water inside the vessel. Carried along on the current of water rushing from the wheelhouse to the sea, Bill surfed to freedom.

"I shot through the door on the flow like a bullet," he says. Moments later, the skipper was able to climb up and join three of his crew on the bottom of the *Morning Dove*.

As soon as he was safe on the hull, Bill took control of the situation again. His first job was to get David from the water and on the boat with them. Although he wondered how long the steel-hulled vessel would stay afloat, he knew that David would be better off with the rest of them. With no time to grab an immersion suit or life jacket before the boat sank, the young crewman, like the others, was dressed in light clothing. Bill knew that David would become hypothermic within minutes if they couldn't get him from the freezing water. Climbing down the side of his overturned vessel, Bill tried to retrieve a life ring in case David drifted nearer to them.

Suddenly he caught a glimpse of a most welcome sight.

"I saw black smoke coming from the smokestacks of a couple of boats about a half-mile away. That's when I knew someone heard my mayday," he says.

Explaining that black smoke meant the vessels had throttled up their engines and were going full speed ahead instead of steaming at the power they use to tow shrimp gear, Bill says he was reminded of June 18, 1992 when his first longliner sank. His emotions were comparable to the sense of relief he felt that day when a Search and Rescue helicopter arrived to where his 47-foot longliner, *Paula and Jordan*, was being battered by heavy seas and high winds.

The *Cape Chadallyn* was the first vessel to arrive. Following Bill's hand-signalled directions, the rescue vessel altered course and headed toward David Reid, still clinging to the wooden table. While David was being pulled from the ocean, another vessel, *A.J. Chaisson*, backed in alongside the nearly submerged hull of the *Morning Dove* and rescued the other four men.

For the second time in his short career as a fishing skipper, lady luck smiled on Bill Dawe. Just as the *Paula and Jordan* sank immediately after the crew was rescued in 1992, the *Morning Dove* ended her *final voyage* and succumbed to the pull of the Labrador Sea as she slipped beneath the surface, just minutes after her five-man crew were safe on board the rescue vessels.

Horrified Onlookers Watch Helplessly as Seas Claim Two Brothers

By the middle of April 1975, 36-year-old Donald McGrath from St. Brides in Placentia Bay was getting fidgety to get back on the water again after the long winter tie-up. But as anxious as Donald was to go fishing that spring, his younger brother, 34-year-old John McGrath, was even more excited. John had recently quit his job as lightkeeper on Cape St. Mary's to go back to a life on the sea.

On Thursday, April 17, the two brothers, along with their teenaged nephew, Francis McGrath, steamed out from St. Bride's on what could be described as a test run before they started gill net fishing for cod a few days later. Donald wanted to check how his 52-foot longliner, *La Bridget,* was performing after the long winter lay up. While he was checking the vessel's engine, hydraulics and other operating systems, Donald also decided that this would be a good opportunity to see if there were any signs of cod fish out around Cape St. Mary's. Seeing a few fish on the vessel's sounder, the men decided to set a couple of nets.

Things went well all day and sometime around suppertime the three men headed for home. Donald heard on the radio that winds were expected to increase significantly overnight and mentioned to his brother that perhaps they should go to Placentia instead of going home. St. Bride's is situated on an open stretch of shoreline fully exposed to Placentia Bay with little or no protective harbour. The small wharf in the community in 1975 was not sufficient for a relatively large 52-foot longliner in a storm. After considering their options, the men decided that they would go to St. Bride's after all. The forecast didn't call for a heavy gale so they figured things should be fine if they moored *La Bridget* just offshore from the wharf for the night. That way the boat would be secure and they could row ashore in their dory.

As predicted, winds increased Thursday night and heavy seas developed with them. Donald McGrath was up early Friday morning, keeping a close eye on his longliner as huge waves, pushed by high winds, literally washed over the deck as she tossed around on her moorings. John McGrath also got up early that morning but decided to go back to bed and wait out the storm.

About 9:00 A.M., John's wife, Annie, woke her husband, saying that she had just seen Donald's truck heading toward the stages down near the boat. Shortly afterwards, John joined his brother. As the brothers talked while carefully watching *La Bridget's* every heaving motion, Francis also dropped by to see what was happening. Afraid that the wooden-hulled longliner had taken on water as a result of seas washing over the hull for several hours, the men decided to go out and pump out the hold. As they prepared to push the dory from the shore, Donald asked Francis to go get some rope that was located on the stage. Shortly after Francis left, the two men realized they already had plenty of rope in the dory and decided to leave without waiting for Francis to return.

When the two men boarded the longliner, they were pleased to find that she hadn't taken on as much water as they had thought. As they pumped the water out of the hold, huge waves continued to crash against the vessel, at times throwing them off balance. The dinner table in the galley had split into two pieces from the violent tossing around.

From shoreline, about 200 feet away, David McGrath watched as his younger brothers climbed over the side of *La Bridget,* back into the dory. David, also a fisherman, was nervous because he didn't have any confidence in the stability of the little boat. He remembered the words of a friend who described it as a "floating coffin." Little did he realize how prophetic that statement was. As David and his fishing partner, John Young, watched, a wave capsized the dory, throwing both John and Donald overboard.

Horrified, David and John frantically tried to find a way to help. Because the fishing season had not begun, all the dories in St. Bride's were still hauled up for winter storage, leaving the men onshore with no way of getting to the McGrath brothers. Helpless, all they could do was stand and watch and pray. David was momentarily relieved when he saw Donald surface and climb up on the bottom of the overturned dory. That relief was short-lived though. Seconds later, another wave struck and washed his brother back into the water again. At the same time, John had managed to grab a steel cable that was tethered to the longliner from the beach. For a while John made some progress in pulling himself toward shore on the cable, but as the longliner lurched in the heavy seas, the cable violently jerked back and forth in the water, eventually striking him in the head. The blow apparently knocked John unconscious, rendering him incapable of fighting the seas anymore.

La Bridget.

Also watching from shore, Fred White remembered an old aban-
doned dory that was hauled up a few hundred feet from where he was
standing. As he saw Donald crawling back on the overturned dory a
second time, Fred ran and pushed the old dory into the water. Using
a piece of board that had been lying on the beach for an oar, he tried
to paddle his way toward his friend but, sadly, Donald couldn't hang
on as another heavy sea swept him back into the ocean. The bitterly
cold waters of April had taken its toll and Donald simply couldn't
find the energy and strength to battle the ocean one more time.

As if satisfied that it had caused enough grief and anguish, the
churning seas suddenly went calm that morning.

"It was just amazing, 20 to 25 minutes later, the ocean was as flat as oil," says Annie McGrath.

David McGrath concurs with his sister-in-law. "You could row out to the longliner in a bathtub. If they had stayed on just a bit longer they wouldn't have had any problem at all," he says, adding that the tragedy was "almost like it was meant to be," for some sad reason.

On April 18, 1975, the fishing season had not even started in earnest in Placentia Bay, but brothers Donald and John McGrath had already made their *final voyage*.

Veteran Skipper Braves Gale to Help
Fisherman in Distress

September 26, 1984 was just another routine Wednesday for lightkeeper Stuart Hancock – at least it was routine until just after 9:00 P.M.

The lightkeeper on evening watch at the Peckford's Island lighthouse in Notre Dame Bay noticed that the winds, which had been strong all day, had become a full-blown southwesterly gale. *It's not a good night to be out in boat*, he thought, staring out the lighthouse residence window at the ominous black clouds and heavy, crashing seas. Aware of the hazards to shipping in this kind of weather, especially for small inshore fishing boats, Stuart kept an attentive ear to both the VHF radio and CB set. At the same time, the experienced lighthouse keeper kept a trained eye towards the ocean, quickly scanning the rough seas for any sign of a vessel in trouble.

Other than the sound of the howling winds and the thunderous seas crashing at the bottom of the cliffs about 100 feet below the lighthouse, everything appeared normal until sometime about 9:15 P.M. At first Stuart wasn't sure if he heard a voice on the CB set or not.

"It was so faint, I wasn't sure if it was my imagination but I thought I heard someone sending a mayday," he says.

Turning up the volume, Stuart heard the barely audible voice again. It was Calvin Waterman, skipper of the longliner *North Queen* out of Twillingate, requesting assistance. The fishing captain explained that the stabilizers on his 55-foot fishing vessel had broken and when the boat started heaving around in the rough seas, the mast collapsed and crashed onto the boat's deck, causing serious damage to the vessel's superstructure.

Stuart Hancock wasted no time calling the Canadian Coast Guard to inform them of the *North Queen's* plight. The lightkeeper explained that the *North Queen* was situated approximately 10 miles southwest of the Funk Islands in Notre Dame Bay. The officer checked the locations of Coast Guard ships and replied there were none in the immediate vicinity, and that it might be better to try to get a fishing vessel to the rescue. He suggested calling Morley Rowe from Fogo Island.

Ironically, Morley Rowe knew only too well the peril the *North Queen* was facing that night. Morley and his crew had just arrived in port on Fogo Island.

"We'd just punched in through that storm and I just got in the house when I got the call from Stuart," he says. Although it was one of the worst nights he'd ever been at sea, the veteran skipper from Seldom didn't hesitate to call his crew back together. After filling the tanks on his 55-foot *Notre Dame Venture* as quickly as he could, Morley was out to sea again before midnight to try and assist a colleague and a friend.

With the strong winds on their stern, the rescue boat was heading toward the stricken vessel at near-record speed.

"We went out there like a squid that night but there were times when she'd bury her head right under," Morley remembers.

On board the *North Queen*, Cal Waterman could only wait and hope and pray that the storm wouldn't get any worse. Although the fallen spar had knocked out lights and some electronics, including his VHF radio, the engine was working properly, allowing the skipper to keep the longliner jogging safely into the wind. Back at the lighthouse, Stuart Hancock would not venture away from the CB radio. "The other lightkeeper, Carson Sturge, used to bring me tea and a snack now and then, while I made sure to keep listening in and calling the boats at least every half hour," he says.

"I was happy to have Stuart checking in all the time on the CB," Cal Waterman remembers today.

Waterman was comforted to have the lightkeeper standing by in case something else went wrong, but he was even happier to see the searchlights of the *Notre Dame Venture* shining through the rain and fog about 3:30 A.M.

"She was a hard sight to look at," Morley Rowe remembers. "The spar was down across her and there was cables and chains all over the place – the wheelhouse was smashed in and, boy oh boy, she was a mess."

Trying to contend with mountainous seas and winds at gale force, both skippers agreed that it was too risky to try to get a line from the *Notre Dame Venture* to the *North Queen* unless it became the last resort. But trying to steam the *North Queen* under her own power presented other challenges. Because several cables and chains were hanging over the side of the vessel into the water, there was a danger of getting them tangled in the prop if they moved too quickly. Moving slowly forward at between one and two knots, Morley and the crew on the *Venture* travelled slightly ahead, providing a wind and sea break for the damaged vessel. For hours, the two longliners fought the winds and seas as they inched their way steadily toward Fogo Island.

Early Thursday morning, the *Notre Dame Venture* and *North Queen* slowly rounded the headland into the calm and safe haven of Cape Cove on Fogo Island.

Back in the lighthouse on Peckford's Island, a tired but happy Stuart Hancock breathed a sigh of relief as he made his way to his bunk, knowing that he had played a significant role in saving the *North Queen* from what could easily have been her *final voyage.*

Cut Down –

Two Cape Sable Island Fishermen Die

"Look out!"

Those were the last words Truman Nickerson ever heard from his older brother Blantford, and from that moment, life for Truman would never be the same.

Late on Friday night, September 12, 1952, Blantford and Truman, along with their cousin Orville, were busy preparing for a halibut fishing trip on the so-called 25-Mile Grounds located 25 miles south-southwest of Cape Sable Island, Nova Scotia. All three Nickersons lived in a small town called The Hawk on Cape Island. About two hours after midnight, the three young fishermen were pulling away from the dock at nearby Swims Point.

As skipper, 27-year-old Blantford took the wheel of his 40-foot Cape Islander *Wizzer*, while Truman and Orville were busy getting last minute things done before arriving at the fishing grounds. The weather was fairly good, as far as winds and seas go, but the fog was mud-thick. As dawn broke, the *Wizzer* was just a few minutes away from the 25-Mile Grounds and as Orville was baiting the last of the trawl lines, 25-year-old Truman went below for a quick breakfast. Just as he was finishing a piece of pie at the end of his breakfast, Truman was startled when he heard his brother scream, "Look out!"

Not sure what was happening, Truman was certain from the tone of Blantford's voice that something was terribly wrong. Rushing to the door to see what was going on, Truman barely had time to blink before he was thrown violently to the side of the boat.

Truman Nickerson is not quite sure what happened during the next few minutes. It happened so quickly that it all seemed like a slow-motion and fragmented dream-like experience. Vaguely aware that the *Wizzer* had been run down by a large ship, and before ending up in the water, he remembered, somewhere along the way, grabbing at Blantford's shirt, but that was all.

Grabbing a wooden keg that was used on fishing gear, Truman kept himself afloat while he yelled for Blantford and Orville. There was no reply and there was no sign of his brother and cousin. Unable to swim, Truman kept calling as he managed to splash his way to some wreckage of the *Wizzer* that was floating nearby. Pulling himself halfway up on a piece of the vessel's bow, Truman couldn't climb any farther. Submerged from the waist down, he waited and prayed that someone would find him.

In fact, several people almost did find Truman that day. Other fishing vessels from Cape Island were also on the way to 25-Mile Grounds that morning and saw pieces of the *Wizzer's* wreckage. Quick to realize that one of their own boats had been run down, the fishermen soon had an impromptu search underway.

Truman heard boats steaming near him several times that day. He yelled and yelled, but no one could hear him over the drone of engines. Although they came very close, nobody saw him because the fog was so thick they needed to be within a couple hundred feet. By afternoon, Truman couldn't even call out anymore. His throat had become so sore from yelling out that his voice was nothing more than a whisper.

It is impossible to describe how desolate and alone Truman Nickerson must have felt that Friday evening when the last sound of boats faded away in the fog. As a fisherman, he knew that his colleagues had gone back to port to wait out the darkness before coming back. In 1952, Nova Scotian Cape Islanders were not equipped with the sophisticated electronics available today. There was no GPS, Loran, radar or VHF and CBs on board. The only navigational aid on most boats was a compass.

Back on Cape Sable Island, word quickly spread about the wreckage of a fishing vessel near 25-Mile Grounds. Fisherman Abner Atwood, next door neighbour to Truman Nickerson, stayed up almost all night pondering tides, weather, winds and every other piece of data that he could gather regarding the past 24 hours. Piecing it all together and adding it to the time he figured the Nickersons were cut down, Abner decided to recreate what he considered to be the final hours of the *Wizzer.* Allowing for tide drifts and currents and the other factors, Abner calculated all the indices, eventually pinpointing the location where he thought that possible survivors would be located.

Saturday morning Abner Atwood took his young son with him and steamed a steady course for near the 25-Mile Grounds.

After 29 hours in the ocean without food or water, Truman Nickerson was hypothermic and a little delirious by noon on Saturday, September 13. That's why he thought he was hallucinating when he saw Abner Atwood's boat steaming straight at him just a few hundred feet away. With his voice still gone, Truman couldn't shout to get Abner's attention but joyfully, he didn't need to do anything. Abner had a clear lead on his neighbour and friend. Within minutes they were headed back to land.

As an interesting sidebar to this amazing story, Abner came perilously close to recreating more of the *Wizzer's* last trip than he needed. A little more than halfway in, Abner saw something large and dark looming through the still-thick fog. For a moment Abner thought he was looking at a cliff, but soon realized that he was still nowhere near land. Suddenly, he recognized the large hull of an Irving Oil tanker. Fortunately, Abner had time to manoeuvre his boat out of harm's way but it was a scary and eerie experience. *How strange*, Abner thought. *Here I am bringing in a man who was cut down and nearly gets cut down myself.* It is unfathomable, of course, to think how Truman would have felt about a second incident in as many days.

Truman lived nearly 45 years after that fateful day, although he never fully recovered from the damage caused by the effects of being in the water for all those hours. He eventually lost the use of his legs and couldn't walk or work for the last 20 or so years of his life.

Blantford Nickerson was a popular young man in his community. His nephew Boyd Nickerson, who now fishes out of Yarmouth, described his uncle as a man who was good at everything he did.

"He was one of those who seemed to be the best at everything – he was a good ball player, he had been in the merchant navy and all that – he was one that stood out." Brantford was also known as a good fisherman.

He left a wife and four children.

Orville Nickerson, 22, was not married.

What happened that day remains a mystery. It is likely that no one on the ship that rammed the *Wizzer* even knew that they had struck anything. Because the 25-Mile Grounds are located in busy shipping lanes, it would have been difficult to pinpoint a single ship within those coordinates at the precise moment of the collision. The only thing certain is that Blantford and Orville Nickerson from *The Hawk*, Cape Sable Island, made their *final voyage* in September 1952.

Fisherman Succumbs after Saving Son and Grandson

Monday, July 5, 1993 was not a nice summer's day in Wesleyville, Bonavista Bay, but a cool eight-degree temperature with mist and overcast skies was not enough to keep lobster fishermen from tending their pots. Neither were the 20-knot easterly winds. It was not a nice day, but it was good enough for veteran fisherman Raymond Howell, his son Dwayne Howell and Raymond's grandson, Chris Goodyear, to haul and reset about 150 lobster pots that morning. Following the morning's work, the three went back home for lunch. After a late lunch they decided to head back out to finish the day's work and reset several more pots.

They left Wesleyville around 3:00 P.M. in their 18-foot open speedboat, intending to move pots located near Green Island to a more productive fishing area near Flowers Island, a short distance away. Their work was only expected to take a couple of hours.

When the three men didn't return home by dusk, their families became worried and notified the RCMP. Despite heavy fog an initial search got under way almost immediately. Since the boat had last been reported fishing around Flowers Island, a radar scan was done in that area but there was no sign of the small boat or any of the three fishermen. Thinking the men may have landed on Flowers Island, searchers checked all the cabins there, but there was still no sign of anyone. Late Monday night, a full-scale search got underway and at daylight Tuesday morning, a group of small open boats joined the effort. Around eleven o'clock that morning, searchers in a small open boat passing Swain Island, more than three miles west of Flowers Island, saw two men on shore waving and shouting. It was Dwayne Howell and Chris Goodyear.

Raymond Howell was not with them.

It seems that for a while everything was going smoothly for the three lobster fishermen on Monday afternoon. Weather conditions had not changed significantly from earlier that day when they worked their pots. Winds had strengthened a bit but seas were not considered to be rough. Shortly after three o'clock the fishermen had reset one lobster pot off the southwest side of Green Island and had four more pots on board ready to be relocated. With the throttle of the 20-horsepower outboard motor less than half open, the skipper, Raymond Howell, manoeuvred the boat slowly to the next position while Dwayne and Craig stood on the lee side of the speedboat with pots ready to be dropped.

Suddenly a large wave hit the high side of the speedboat, capsizing it immediately, throwing all three men overboard. Raymond Howell was able to climb onto the bottom of the overturned boat and somehow managed to haul Dwayne and Chris, neither of whom could swim, from the ocean and onto the boat with him. When all three were safely out of the water, they adjusted their sitting positions on the boat's keel to keep it as stable as possible. The experienced fishermen knew that it was important to keep the boat from attempting to right itself because if she turned even slightly to an upright position the boat would probably sink, leaving Raymond, Dwayne and Chris without any support.

For a little while it appeared that things might work out, but shortly after they seemed to have gained some control of their situation, Raymond appeared to suddenly lose consciousness and was washed overboard by a wave. Without a life jacket or any flotation device, Raymond disappeared beneath the surface before the other two had a chance to help him. Investigators suspect the 59-year-old fisherman became exhausted in his struggle to assist his son and grandson and simply couldn't hold on any longer.

The next five hours were the most terrifying time in the lives of Dwayne Howell and Chris Goodyear. The two men constantly shifted positions to keep the boat stable as they drifted in a southwesterly direction. Fortunately, a piece of rope and an oar floated out from underneath the capsized boat. They used the rope to secure themselves more safely to the boat and also to each other, and then took turns paddling with the oar to keep the boat from drifting broadside to the seas, which could wash them overboard again.

On several occasions during their ordeal, the two men heard boats passing in the distance, but they had no means of summoning help. At times, both Chris and Dwayne felt they would not survive, but panic attacks were limited by their concern for each other. At one point, one of the men realized they were drifting toward Swain Island and, if they held on long enough, the drifting boat would take them near shore. Knowing that land wasn't far away also helped keep fear and panic at bay. Steadily working the oar, while constantly moving themselves around on the boat's bottom generated enough body heat to stave off hypothermia in the frigid waters. Around eight o'clock Monday evening, just as a heavy fog set in, the boat drifted onto the rocks of Swain Island and the two men managed to struggle ashore.

Although the two fishermen were safe on land, their ordeal was far from over. Cold, soaked, bruised, scared and suffering from early stages of hypothermia, the two could find no shelter on the island, nor was there any material to light a fire to keep warm. The heavy fog was now accompanied by rain and the only thing they could do was huddle in the meagre shelter of a rock crevice.

Early Tuesday morning, Chris and Dwayne heard boats passing in the distance. At first they wondered why the boats were so far from shore. Their hopes of being rescued began to fade when they realized the search was concentrated in the Flowers Island area. That meant all the boats were passing right by Swain Island without checking the shoreline where they were located. With no flares or any other way of attracting attention to themselves, Dwayne and Chris were rapidly weakening and becoming discouraged. Hungry, tired, wet and very cold, they had all but given up hope, when at eleven o'clock they saw a boat not far from shore. Summoning every last ounce of strength in their bodies, Dwayne and Chris managed to climb to their feet and began shouting and frantically waving their arms. Luckily, the men in the boat saw them and within minutes Dwayne and Chris were on their way to hospital.

An hour and a half later, RCMP divers recovered the body of Raymond Howell near Green Island.

Dwayne Howell and Chris Goodyear spent the next 10 days in hospital but made a full recovery from their 20-hour ordeal.

Sadly though, for Raymond Howell, it was his *final voyage.*

Rain Distorts Radar – Tragedy Follows

Life was full of promise for the skipper and four young crew members of the longliner *Andrea Denise* in 1984. Bruce Button was skipper of the 58-footer owned by Quinlan Brothers Ltd. out of Bay de Verde, Trinity Bay. His crew of Garfield (Garf) Bursey, Warren Cooper, Roland Driscoll and Randy Bursey ranged in ages from 22 to 30. At 29, Bruce was one of the youngest skippers of a vessel that size in his area. The five young fishermen were among the first to fish crab more than 50 miles offshore.

The *Andrea Denise* had a good summer's fishery in 1984. By mid-September, catch rates had suddenly dropped in the area where they had been fishing. Because fall was fast approaching, Bruce and the crew decided to move their crab pots closer to land and fish for another few weeks before ending their season.

On Wednesday, September 19, they steamed to the offshore grounds, retrieved their crab gear and headed back to port in Old Perlican. The trip home was uneventful for several hours. By late night it had started raining, at times heavily, and there was a stiff breeze from the southeast creating choppy seas, but nothing that the *Andrea Denise* couldn't handle. Warren Cooper, who was on watch until approximately 1:30 A.M. on Thursday, remembers catching momentary glimpses of the lighthouse on Baccalieu Island, but for the most part rain obscured visibility to just a few feet in front of the vessel.

Shortly before 2:00 A.M., Roland took over on watch as Warren lay down on a small bunk in the wheelhouse. A few minutes later, Warren bolted upright when he heard Roland calling anxiously to the skipper.

"Bruce, it's gone pitch black and I can't see anything on the radar. Can you come up?" Apparently, the heavy rain, by then coming down in sheets, had totally distorted the radar image, blotting out the outline of land not far away.

Within seconds, Bruce Button was in the wheelhouse but before he could consider a new course of action, the *Andrea Denise* struck something.

"We heard a loud thump and then two louder thumps as the boat shook. We knew then we were in trouble," says Warren Cooper.

Luckily, no one got hurt when the vessel struck the rocks, because the men would need every ounce of strength they had if they were to survive the ordeal that followed. Despite the chaos and the dreadful knowledge that the vessel was probably sinking, the skipper managed to get out a mayday and sent a distress call to a longliner that he knew was about eight miles behind them. Lewellyn Riggs heard the call the first time which was lucky, because there would be no chance for Bruce Button to make a second attempt – the *Andrea Denise* was quickly foundering on the rocks of Baccalieu Island.

While Lewellyn relayed the mayday to the Coast Guard, Bruce, Warren, Randy, Garf and Roland were hurriedly preparing to abandon ship while they still had time. Bruce braved the high winds and seas and climbed to the roof of the wheelhouse to get a life raft ready.

Despite being tossed around by large waves washing across the boat, he somehow held on and got the raft down to the deck. As crab pots, ropes and debris swirled and crashed around the deck of the stricken longliner, the men finally got the life raft off the boat to what they hoped would be safety.

They were wrong.

Try as they would, the men could not manoeuvre the raft towards the open sea, away from the rocks. With strong southeasterly winds pushing them dangerously close to the rocks, the men knew they were faced with a high probability of being smashed against the cliffs where they knew death would be instantaneous. With that grim reality running through their minds, Warren and Bruce decided to jump from the raft as it washed once again across the deck of the *Andrea Denise*.

Back on board the longliner, the two tried to make it to the galley where the life jackets were stowed. With water up to their waists, it was not an easy task. Warren nearly got sucked down through an open hatch into the engine room, the worst place to be under the circumstances. Reaching to grab something to steady himself in the turmoil, Warren unknowingly grabbed the wiring to the VHF radio.

"It was only thirty-two volts, but filled with water, it fried me pretty good," he says. But electrical shock was a minor detail then. As the boat heaved and tossed on the rocks, the mast came crashing down.

"That's when I knew it was time for prayers," says Warren today.

Throughout the chaos, Bruce and Warren caught an occasional glimpse of the life raft washing back and forth under the bow of the longliner, just feet from the cliffs. They could see Garf and Randy clinging to the inflated sides of the raft, the only parts of the rubber craft that remained intact. Miraculously, they had not been crushed to pieces. There was no sign of Roland, who had either been washed from the raft or decided to jump in hopes of gaining greater security. He didn't make it.

After pounding against the rocks for 10 or 12 minutes, the *Andrea Denise* rose high against the cliffs and came down hard. After a movement that Warren describes today as "an *ogeous* great slam," the 58-foot fishing vessel turned into a mass of splinters in front of their eyes.

Despite large and small pieces of wreckage, along with crab pots and fishing gears heaving around in foaming seas, the men somehow surfaced relatively unscathed. Scrambling to grab anything that floated, Bruce and Warren clung to a piece of plywood. Moments later, the waves pushed them alongside Garf Bursey who had been thrown from the life raft. There was no sign of Randy Bursey who had earlier decided to attempt swimming to shore.

Suddenly, as if in answer to their prayers, a strange calm came over the waters near Southeast Baccalieu. Apparently, when the *Andrea Denise* split apart, the fuel tanks ruptured and hundreds of gallons of fuel rose to the surface and smoothed the angry seas. The temporary calm allowed the three men time to move farther offshore, away from danger of being tossed against the rocks.

In spite of the relative safety of the open sea, the three survivors still faced grave danger. Sometime during the night the wind had changed to a strong northwesterly, driving them quickly away from where search parties would concentrate on looking for them. It was also very cold. Drenched, they knew it would not be long before hypothermia would become a serious problem. Considering the odds of surviving, Bruce figured that the small piece of board they were on was unable to support the three men for very long. He decided that he'd better find another piece of debris. It was a tough decision, but he felt it was the best thing for everyone, especially for his buddies.

After drifting for what seemed like an eternity, daylight broke about 6:30 A.M. and, although dazed by the cold, Warren and Garf were still conscious. The two men kept nudging each other awake when the desire to sleep became overwhelming. Just after daylight, the cargo ship *Astron* steamed by very close to the survivors. Fortunately, the *Astron's* cook caught a glimpse of them and alerted the captain. Within minutes, a Search and Rescue helicopter was hovering above Garf and Warren. Hoisted on board the helicopter by SAR technicians on swinging cables, both Warren and Garf immediately informed their rescuers that their skipper should be somewhere nearby. The technicians apparently had seen Bruce – he appeared lifeless. So they had worked first with the two men who were obviously alive, intending to get the third victim afterwards.

He had appeared lifeless, but the young captain of the *Andrea Denise* was not dead. Although unconscious and suffering from advanced hypothermia, Bruce Button was alive, and within minutes he too had been successfully hoisted from a small piece of debris to the safety of the SAR helicopter.

After a short stay at the Health Sciences Centre in St. John's, Bruce Button, Warren Cooper and Garf Bursey made a full recovery. Sadly, Roland Driscoll and Randy Bursey had made their *final voyage* on September 20, 1984.

Labrador Man Drowns with Rescuers Just Moments Away

Life was good for Douglas Fowler in the summer of 1993. Despite facing a newly imposed moratorium on northern cod fishing, Douglas, a fisherman from Capstan Island, Labrador, was luckier than many of his Labrador Straits colleagues. Fishing with his brothers Dorman and George, along with George's son Christopher, Douglas hoped to put together a successful season fishing for scallops on board Dorman's longliner, *Jason and Jamie.* Like his brothers and nephew, Douglas was determined to make the best of whatever the seas would allow that summer. With a wife and young daughter at home in Capstan Island, Douglas had plenty of incentive to work.

On Monday morning, July 26, exactly two weeks after his thirty-third birthday, Douglas, along with his two brothers and nephew, was eager for an early start to the fishing day. It was a perfect summer morning, and by 4:30 A.M. all four Fowler men were on board the *Jason and Jamie*, which was docked at the wharf in L'Anse au Clair.

Following the usual pre-fishing preparations, the Fowlers were soon steaming to the scallop grounds about 10 miles from L'Anse au Clair.

"You could see your face in the water that day, that's how calm it was," says Dorman Fowler, skipper of the 45-foot longliner. With ideal weather conditions forecast for the remainder of the day, the four fishermen were in an upbeat mood as they fished through the morning.

Shortly after noon, Dorman received a call on VHF radio from a nearby scalloper. It seems the neighbouring fishing vessel was running dangerously low on fuel, and rather than try steaming back to port, the skipper wondered if Dorman could help him out. Pulling alongside his friend's boat, Dorman ran a drain line from the *Jason and Jamie's* fuel tanks and pumped 20 gallons of fuel to the other vessel, something that would have been impossible in choppy seas.

After performing their good deed for the day, the Fowlers continued scallop dragging and, as in the morning, the fishing was pretty good. It wasn't the best fishing they'd ever seen, but then neither was it discouraging.

About 2:00 P.M. Dorman engaged the hydraulic system to start taking back the scallop bucket with the results of another tow. Ordinarily, when the scallop gear broke through the surface, Christopher and Douglas, standing on the aft deck, would each hook the cable hoists with a gaff. After guiding the 5,000 pounds of iron chains, bar and bucket in over the deck with the gaffs, the men would release the scallops on board the vessel. Because the *Jason and Jamie* was sitting perfectly still in the flat calm waters in the Labrador Straits that July day, both Douglas and Christopher decided to climb up on the ramp on the stern of the vessel and guide the scallop bucket in over the deck with their hands.

In the wheelhouse, Skipper Dorman Fowler decided to take a look at how the take-back procedure was going.

"I walked back through the galley and had just leaned on the bottom half of the galley door leading to the deck when all of a sudden the hydraulic hose broke," Dorman remembers. When the hose that supplied pressure to the scallop gear hoisting cables broke, the large iron scallop bucket suddenly dropped back into the ocean, causing the idling 45-foot longliner to lurch forward. Christopher Fowler managed to hang on to a piece of gear on the ramp, but his uncle Douglas was knocked off-balance and was thrown from the ramp into the ocean.

Dorman knew his brother wasn't wearing a life jacket and he also knew Douglas couldn't swim. Deeply concerned and troubled by the fear that his brother might panic, Dorman wasted no time in getting to the wheelhouse, kicking the hydraulics system out of gear with his foot on the way forward. Hauling the rudder hard to the starboard, Dorman opened the engine full speed and began circling back toward the position where he had just seen Douglas frantically smacking the water with both hands, trying to tread water and stay above the surface. At the same time as he spun the wheel, Dorman grabbed the VHF radio microphone and quickly alerted other boats in the area that he had a "man overboard."

Because the scallop grounds in the Labrador Straits are concentrated in a relatively small area, dozens of vessels fish within a few hundred feet of one another.

"We often shout short conversations back and forth while we're towing, we're that close," Dorman says. Within a couple of minutes, a dozen scallop boats, coming from all directions, were speeding toward Douglas. Most vessels had men standing on top of the wheelhouses where they could maintain the best possible view of the man in the water. To everyone's astonishment, Douglas Fowler was suddenly nowhere to be seen.

"One second he was there, flousin' around in the water and then suddenly, nothing," Dorman remembers. Boats slowed to a halt near where Douglas was last seen. An eerie silence descended over all the fishermen as they swept experienced, searching eyes over the water, watching and waiting to see Douglas rise back to the surface.

"They say people go down three times before they drown but we don't believe he went down more than once," Dorman says.

They never saw the young fisherman again.

Hundreds of Newfoundland and Labrador fishermen have drowned, but seldom has anyone disappeared as quickly as Douglas Fowler did that day when help and safety was, literally, just a few feet away.

Many people wonder if Douglas might have been struck and injured by the scallop gear when the hydraulics broke and the bucket fell. His brothers and Christopher, who witnessed the accident at close range, all agree that the gear did not hit Douglas and he didn't strike his head while falling from the boat. Most people, including Dorman, believe that Douglas simply panicked and couldn't stay afloat long enough for anyone to reach him. Without the body available to determine whether he had suffered an injury, only one thing is certain today. On Monday, July 26, 1993, 33-year-old Douglas Fowler from Capstan Island, Labrador, made his *final voyage* to the Labrador Straits.

Is It Fred or Is It Brett?

"Is it Fred or is it Brett?"

Those were the words Eva Wareham muttered intuitively when she opened the front door to her St. John's home one afternoon in June 1974, and saw Reverend Babb standing there. The solemn look on the minister's face that day told Eva that something terrible had happened and, somehow, she knew that it involved either her husband, Fred, a fisherman, or her son Brett who was a schoolteacher in Buchans at the time.

Knowing that her husband had gone to haul his salmon nets so that he could save the fishing gear from fast-approaching ice, Eva immediately feared the worst. Her instincts were correct.

"It's Fred," said Reverend Babb, softly.

The spring of 1974 produced some of the worst ice conditions on record on the east coast of Newfoundland. Hundreds of fishermen along the coastline had tens of thousands of dollars worth of fishing nets and lobster pots destroyed by large chunks of ice that kept moving in and off the fishing grounds for weeks. Fishermen like Fred Wareham from St. John's had to be constantly vigilant to ensure that he didn't become one of the unfortunate ones.

Early Monday morning, June 17, Fred and his crewmen Pat Doyle and George Abbot hauled their salmon nets near Blackhead Point, about three miles from the St. John's Narrows. Although the wind was "in" from the dreaded northeast, the ice was a long distance offshore that morning, so Skipper Fred decided it was safe to set the nets again, figuring that they would check on the ice conditions later in the afternoon. If the ice had moved closer to Blackhead, he could call Pat and George and they'd simply go out and take the nets in for the night. But the currents and winds were pushing the ice at a much faster pace than even the experienced 59-year-old Fred Wareham had calculated. The three fishermen had barely made it back home when someone phoned and said the ice was rapidly moving south and would soon be closing in on Blackhead and Freshwater Bay. Fred knew he had no time to waste. George and Pat met their skipper on the wharf on the south side of St. John's Harbour, and within minutes the three were once again steaming out through the Narrows in Fred's 38-foot longliner, *Barry Carl*.

Fred Wareham.

With the stiff northeasterly wind growing stronger, Fred probably wished that he had taken in the gear after they hauled it that morning. But then, the cod fishery had not been good in the previous few summers, and salmon was one of the major species that he and the crew depended on to make a successful voyage in 1974. Steaming toward Blackhead as quickly as the *Barry Carl* could travel, Fred was determined to save his 15 salmon nets from ice damage.

"Dad would almost rather lose a finger than have holes torn in his nets," says his son Brett.

Brett remembers his father as a hard-working fisherman who came from a long line of St. John's Warehams who chose life on the sea as their vocation. Known to everyone as a happy, upbeat person, Fred Wareham was a small, wiry man who always wore a quiff hat and a tie, a man who took great pride in his work and a man who always worked hard. Brett says he is certain that his father worked with too much haste that day. That's just the way Fred was in situations like that.

Arriving at the fishing grounds, Fred, Pat and George were relieved to see that the ice had not yet reached their nets. Working as fast as they could to get to the other nets as quickly as possible, Gorge and Pat went "below" to the fish hold to stow the twine and ropes properly, as Fred prepared to haul the first net from the water. To save time, Fred put the "gurdy," a mechanical device used to haul nets, on full speed.

Because Pat and George were both below deck in the fish hold, no one saw what happened next, but Brett Wareham, who had fished many times with his dad, is pretty sure how the scene played out.

"I know what dad was like," he says. Brett says Fred was almost certainly standing on top of a table where the gurdy was located, and as the net was coming in, he was directing it down the chute to the fish hold for George and Pat to stow away. Somehow, Fred became entangled in the nets, and with the gurdy operating at full power, there was no time for him to grab the lever and stop the motor. Within seconds, Fred was wrapped around the gear until his head brought up solid against the chute, breaking his neck instantly. By the time George and Pat came up from below to see what had slowed the nets from coming down the chute, Fred's lifeless body was lying on the deck of the longliner.

"I don't know if it's any consolation or not, but his death was instantaneous," Brett says.

Sadly, what was to have been an evening of celebration in the Wareham household turned into an evening of tragedy and sorrow. Fred Wareham made his *final voyage* on the day of his fifty-ninth birthday, June 17, 1974.

A Poor Way to Start the Year

"If you don't go fishing on New Year's Day, it's an awful poor way to start the new year." That was Henry Petten's simple, but philosophical, work ethic. The Port de Grave fisherman repeated it a thousand times and he lived by it from the day he started fishing with his father when he was 12 years old.

And he almost died by it.

Thursday, January 1, 1948, was cold and blustery with a fairly stiff northeast breeze of 25 knots. Determined to start the new year according to his self-prescribed philosophy, 37-year-old Henry and his cousin and fishing partner, Edgar Petten, decided to tend to their trawl lines that morning in an area known locally as the Norther' Ledge, about three miles northeast of Green Point lighthouse. The cold northeast wind and choppy seas made it uncomfortable working from their 30-foot decked trap boat, but otherwise the morning was uneventful. The two cousins finished fishing by noon and headed back to port in Hibbs Cove. About a mile east of Green Point, Henry saw a turr just ahead of the boat. Thinking the bird would make a fine supper, Henry went forward to get his gun while Edgar took over on the tiller. Trying to get positioned to get a good shot at the turr, by then nearly broadside, Henry started to walk to the stern of the boat to get a better shot. Keeping his eye fixed on the bird, Henry wasn't paying close attention to where he was stepping. Just as he was walking by the engine housing, he slipped on the icy deck and, before he knew it, he was overboard.

Like Henry, Edgar was focused on the turr, which then was behind the boat, and didn't realize for a moment what had happened until he saw Henry in the water. Quickly assessing his options, Edgar decided that it would take too long to circle around. "No one could last that long in bitterly cold water in January," he thought. Knowing it was difficult to reverse a running eight-horsepower Acadia make-and-break engine, Edgar figured that backing up the boat was the only way. It worked. The engine reversed and although this was the fastest way, it was still taking a long time getting back to Henry because of the brisk winds. In the meantime, Henry was growing numb in the bone-chilling cold waters, and grew weary of struggling to keep above the waves. He remembered a news story he'd heard that morning about two fishermen from Bonavista Bay who had recently drowned. *I guess it's my turn to drown today*, he thought.

Edgar anxiously watched Henry bobbing in the water until he went down for the third time. Horrified, Edgar kept his eyes fixed on the place where he last saw his cousin. Finally, after what seemed an eternity, Edgar somehow managed to manoeuvre the boat directly to the spot where he last saw Henry sinking beneath the surface. But there was no sign of his fishing partner. It was a long shot but, realizing he didn't have a lot of options, Edgar grabbed the 14-foot spread, a long pole that was used to spread the boat's sail, and rammed it underwater. Then the first of what would be a series of miracles that day occurred – the spread struck Henry in the stomach.

The impact of the pole jogged Henry's senses enough that, although weakened and confused, he grabbed the spread as Edgar started pulling him to the surface. It all reminded Henry of the time he fell overboard once before, when he was a sealer on the *Neptune* in the early 1940s. That time, Henry fell in the freezing waters between ice floes, but fortunately he was able to grab a rope that trailed from the side of the sealing ship and managed to pull himself back to safety. This time it was different. This time Henry was in a rapidly progressing state of hypothermia, making it impossible to do any more than hold on to the spread. Try as he could, Edgar couldn't get Henry up over the side of the trap boat. Exasperated and afraid of losing his friend, Edgar said a prayer.

"Lord, you've got to help me," he said, marshalling all his resources to give it one last try.

Edgar said he was never sure of exactly what happened next. He grabbed the spread and hauled as hard as he could. The next thing he

Pettens – Poor way to start a year. Illustration by Ian Williams.

remembered, Henry was standing in front of him in the boat. Although Edgar knew his cousin had just come through a close brush with death, he couldn't help smiling because "Henry was just standing there holding his false teeth in his hand."

Not caring to be called a hero, Edgar Petten always described saving Henry from his *final voyage* that New Year's Day, in the simplest of terms.

It was a miracle.

Fire at Sea – Fishermen's Nightmare

In his 40 years fishing, Eric Miller has had a few close calls on the water. But the fisherman from Grand Bank still talks about the closest time he ever came to watching colleagues die violently at sea.

Eric and his friend Sid Hillier from Fortune spent the summer of 1980 pair trawling in their 52-foot draggers. Pair trawling is when two vessels tow one trawl between them.

In early June, Sam Durnford took over as captain on the *Sharon Jean* from Sid who took a few weeks off to complete a series of medical tests in hospital in St. John's.

Friday, June 4 was a nice day on Fortune Bay. There was a 15- to 20-knot southwest wind but not enough to pose a problem for vessels like the *Max and Maxine* and *Sharon Jean.* After a good day fishing near Brunette Island, the two vessels took back their fishing gear around 7:30 P.M. and prepared to head for port in Fortune, just minutes away. As Eric went below for a cup of tea, his brother George was working on the fishing gear while another brother, Sim, took the wheel.

Eric had barely taken a sip of tea when Sim called out from the wheelhouse that there seemed to be something wrong with the *Sharon Jean.*

"It looks like steam or smoke coming from Sid's boat," Sim shouted. By the time Eric got to the wheelhouse from the galley, it was obvious that it was not steam coming from the stack. It was definitely smoke. Eric immediately tried to contact Sam on VHF radio, but there was no reply.

"I knew then there was something really wrong," Eric said. He was right. While Eric and his brothers peered at the vessel more intently, wondering what to do next, there appeared to be an explosion in the engine room of the *Sharon Jean*. The Millers were still too far away to know if there was a noise, but they could clearly see long streaks of fire coming through the stack, shooting as far as the top of the mast.

It was about that time when Oliver Hillier, the second crew member on the *Sharon Jean* realized there was a problem. The son of the vessel's owner was back aft stowing fish away when he first saw the flames. Up in the wheelhouse, Sam was unaware of anything wrong until Oliver shouted that there must be a fire in the engine room. Sam immediately tried cutting power to the engine but nothing happened. He pulled back the lever to stop the motor, but the electrical system had already burnt some of the wires, and although the engine slowed a little bit, it kept running at nearly full speed. Running from the wheelhouse to check what was going on, the young skipper met flames leaping from all sides.

On board the *Max and Maxine*, Eric Miller and his two brothers were now close enough to see that Sam and Oliver were in big trouble and needed to get off the *Sharon Jean* as soon as possible. An experienced volunteer firefighter, Eric grabbed a fire extinguisher and ran forward, while George took over on the wheel. Expecting to see the burning vessel slowing down any moment, Eric prepared to jump on board and fight the blaze. But there was a problem. Flames had quickly spread to the wheelhouse, preventing anyone from getting inside. With the engine running at nearly full speed, Eric was facing more than a burning boat; he was also dealing with a vessel totally out of control.

Barely able to keep pace with the runaway dragger, Eric knew it was going to be tricky getting alongside to get Sam and Oliver on board his boat. The *Sharon Jean,* by then, following nothing but the whims of currents and winds, was zigzagging recklessly across Fortune Bay. There was only one way to attempt a rescue.

"Our only hope was to ram her," Eric explains. "What we had to do was aim for the slaughterhouse and hope to stay alongside long enough to get one or both of them on board our boat." It didn't work that way. Just as they struck the dragger, a large power-block on the stern of the *Sharon Jean* hooked the railing on the *Max and Maxine* ripping the wood to pieces. Although he was close enough to the rescue boat to jump, Oliver was overwhelmed by the sight and sound of two 30-ton vessels crashing together.

Knowing there were only a few seconds of opportunity, Eric tried to shock the young man into jumping.

"I roared at him," Eric laughs today. "You gotta' jump or else you'll f'n die. Now, take your pick." At that moment the seas rolled the *Max and Maxine* closer to the burning vessel, allowing Eric and Sam to reach over the twisted railing and grab Oliver, plucking him to safety.

Still steaming at nearly full speed, the two vessels finally sheared away. Sam shouted that he wanted to jump overboard but Eric thought that was too dangerous because Sam couldn't get inside the wheelhouse to get a life jacket. "I shouted back that I wanted to try to ram the boat one more time. "Get ready to jump on board!" Eric shouted as George swung the *Max and Maxine* at the burning vessel once again.

It was a scary moment for Sam. Watching a 52-foot dragger just a few feet away bearing straight down at him was not a pretty sight, but just as the two boats struck, Sam timed his jump perfectly. A few seconds later he landed safely on the deck of Eric's boat without receiving a scratch.

Timing is everything, as they say. Just a couple of minutes after Sam landed on Eric's boat, flames ignited the gas tanks on the *Sharon Jean*.

Fire at sea. Illustration by Ian Williams..

"She was just one holy light," Eric says, looking out his window at the location where it happened. The rest of the night was spent watching the burning wreck, until she finally sank the next morning just off Fortune on her *final voyage.*

Four Brothers and Friend Perish in Sudden Winter Storm

Henry Reid had seen worse storms in his 28 years as keeper of the Cape Anguille lighthouse near Codroy on Newfoundland's west coast, but he had never seen one come on so quickly as the winter storm on January 24, 1987. On CBC Television's *Land & Sea* program, the veteran lightkeeper claimed, "It came out of nowhere; within minutes it struck – it was almost too bad for a human to stand up."

Although the storm was forecast, it was the fact that it hit with such sudden ferocity that caused one of Newfoundland's best-known inshore fishing disasters, the loss of the *Myers III.*

Four brothers and a friend perished that day, just minutes away from port in Codroy. Brothers Joe, aged 37; Clarence, 36; Dave, 34; and Jim Myers, 31, all from Bartlett's Harbour along with a young friend, 21-year-old Ewan Hynes from nearby Reef's Harbour, died when their 45-foot inshore dragger sank.

As in most cases when there are no survivors, no one knows for sure what happened that fateful day. Everything was going well on the fishing grounds until about suppertime that evening. Under the command of Joe Myers, the four brothers and Ewan Hynes left port in Codroy that morning, sometime between five and seven o'clock. Ewan was an inshore fisherman who decided to go on the trip "just for a ride."

They had plenty of company as nine other fishing vessels left Codroy around the same time, all headed for the fishing grounds just six or seven miles to the west. By mid-morning several of those vessels reported sighting the *Myers III* fishing nearby. About 11:00 A.M. the *Myers III* called the vessel *Rich Point* on VHF radio. Everything was fine then. Skipper Joe Myers reported a catch of 10,000 pounds of fish in the first set that morning. Nearly two hours later, at 12:45 P.M., in another radio contact with the *Rich Point*, he reported another 10,000-pound catch. The results of both catches were verified in a radio conversation with another vessel, *Oderin*, a short while later, at approximately 1:30 P.M. That was the last radio contact from the *Myers III* although the *Oderin* made several attempts to reach them later that afternoon. No one thought much about the fact that they couldn't make radio contact, because the skipper of the *Myers III* had mentioned something about a 'short' in the back of the VHF set.

Although there was no radio contact, there were several sightings of the *Myers III* in the afternoon. At four o'clock the *Michael J II* saw them hauling in another catch, and as late as 5:40 P.M. the

117

skipper on the *Oderin* saw the *Myers III* on radar, still about six miles west of Codroy. Just minutes before that radar contact, winds had picked up from 20 knots and quickly moved up to 50 to 60 knots from the southwest. At the same time, the barometer had rapidly dropped from 30.3 to 29 inches, indicating that bad weather was approaching. At that time, all the other boats had quit fishing and headed to port. There was no reason to believe the *Myers III* didn't do the same.

Man in submerged wheelhouse. Illustration by Ian Williams.

All the other vessels had safely arrived at port by 7:00 P.M. except two. The *Myers III* and the *Barry & Trina* didn't make it. Unlike the *Myers III*, the *Barry & Trina* did make landfall just southeast of Codroy but foundered on the rocks there. All of the crew members were rescued.

A search for the stricken vessels started early that night, but gale-force winds and limited visibility in blowing snow hampered the search. However, one of the vessels tasked to the scene reported momentarily seeing the mast lights of a vessel approximately one and a half miles south of Codroy Island. In all likelihood it was the *Myers III*, because on May 26, the wreck of the vessel was found on the bottom in a hundred feet of water very close to that location.

The guessing game continues to this day about exactly what happened. Only two bodies were found and since both were wearing light clothing and without life jackets, investigators believe the vessel was suddenly overwhelmed, with no time for an orderly abandonment. There are still some critics who say the small dragger stayed too long on the fishing grounds and was overloaded – it was estimated the *Myers III* had about 48,000 pounds of fish on board. Fishermen bristle at that notion. They claim that the skipper and crew of the *Myers III* did nothing that other fishermen don't do every day. "It was just the luck of the draw," they contend.

Luck of the draw or not, the sad truth is that four enterprising young brothers from one small northeast coastal community, along with an even younger friend from next door are gone forever as the result of the *final voyage* of the *Myers III*.

Uncle Tom Survived It All

He has been robbed at knifepoint, he came face to face with a polar bear once and he laughs about the time his fishing boat was stalked by a German submarine, but Uncle Tom Hatcher will never forget the night of August 2, 1945.

"It was one of the finest nights since the world was made," the 80-something retired fisherman muses, looking out his kitchen window in Rose Blanche. Just after 10:00 P.M., Tom and five other crew members of the fishing vessel *Ethel and Albert* were seven miles from the fairway buoy in North Sydney, steaming to the cod grounds. Tom, Morris Banfield, Sam Harris and Jack Sheppard, skipper and owner of the 20-ton "jackboat," were sleeping. George Best poured a cup of tea as he prepared to relieve Jim Hatcher on watch. Before Jim went below deck for the night, he and George chatted about fishing and the weather, especially the beautiful night they were enjoying.

"You can see for miles but the only thing in sight is the light of a steamer a couple miles behind us, apparently headed for Port aux Basques," Jim said to George. Because the night was so clear, there was no concern about the approaching steamship. The *Ethel and Albert* was appropriately lighted and nothing more was said about it. Because it was such a warm night, Jim decided to stay up for a while.

"It's too warm to go the bunk tonight so I think I'll lie down out here on the locker," he said to George, as he went to the galley to pour a mug of tea. That was the most fortuitous decision Jim Hatcher ever made. Before he had time to finish his mug-up, the stem of the SS *Burgeo* came slicing straight through the bow of the *Ethel and Albert* at a 90-degree angle exactly where his head would have been in the bunk.

Just a few feet away, Tom Hatcher was thrown violently from his bunk. Rushing to the deck of the small schooner, Tom remembers seeing what appeared to be a wall of lights.

"Bright lights, and lots of them," he said.

Fearing a German navy vessel had run down their boat, Tom dashed to the engine room to get a dry cell battery.

"I thought we were struck by a navy boat and I wasn't going to have any part of getting on board a warship, so I was heading for the lifeboat, intent on rowing to North Sydney. I was getting the battery to operate a light," he recalls.

Amazingly, none of the crew was hurt. They wasted no time in getting a lifeboat over the side, but when the *Burgeo* backed away from the schooner, water came gushing in through the hole, leaving no time to retrieve their belongings. Once in the lifeboat, Tom and his shipmates realized the passenger steamer was not a warship. Feeling a little better, they accepted the invitation to climb the rope ladder to safety instead of rowing to shore. By the time the last of the six fishermen had stepped onto the deck of the *Burgeo,* the *Ethel and Albert* was slipping beneath the surface.

The crew of the small fishing schooner was thankful nothing worse happened that August night in 1945. But more than 50 years later, Tom Hatcher is still angry about it. As far as he's concerned the

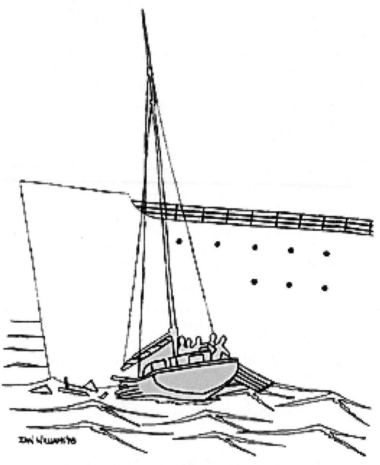

Uncle Tom (Hatcher) has seen it all. Illustration by Ian Williams.

incident should never have happened. According to Tom, one of the passengers on the *Burgeo* even called out to the fellow on watch asking why they were headed straight for the schooner.

"That was several minutes before the collision, which gave them lots of time to clear the boat by a half mile or more," Tom says, shaking his head in disgust. "There were rumours that the man on watch on the *Burgeo* had been drinking, but I don't know if that's true or not and, of course, we'll never know."

The loss of the schooner was one thing, but Tom Hatcher is still upset about the treatment they received after the incident. Although they were just minutes away from their home in North Sydney, Captain Gullage of the *Burgeo* decided to continue the trip to Port aux Basques, and although the fishermen were given food and a place to sleep, they were not able to get home until two days later. And what irks Tom Hatcher most is that they lost all their provisions and, perhaps more importantly, the rest of the fishing season for no reason, and were not able to get any help.

"I checked with a lawyer in Sydney, and he told me we couldn't sue the King's steamship so we might just as well forget it."

Tom Hatcher didn't go back fishing anymore after that summer and, even though he's retired, he still wonders what might have happened to his life if August 2, 1945 had not been the *final voyage* for the *Ethel and Albert.*

Red Paint Raises Questions

Thursday night, May 12, 1988 was a pretty routine evening for fishermen Cecil Strickland from Point au Gaul and Peter Henneburry from Lord's Cove. The two life-long buddies from the Burin Peninsula were having their regular nightly telephone conversation about fishing, the weather and other odds and ends, but the conversation lasted a little longer than usual that night because Cecil had some news for Peter. Cecil was telling Peter all about the brand new speedboat that Cecil's younger brother Andre had just bought. Cecil and Andre, who lived in nearby Allan's Island, were fishing partners, so the conversation centred on the new fibreglass boat and the new 60-horsepower Yamaha outboard motor that came with it.

"I don't know if we should take her out for the first run tomorrow or not," Cecil said.

"Why not?" Peter wanted to know.

"Because tomorrow is Friday the thirteenth," Cecil laughed. Peter laughed too, but replied that he was superstitious and there was no way he would christen a new boat on Friday the thirteenth. Cecil allowed that he and Andre didn't believe in that "old stuff" and that they would probably head out first thing in the morning.

That was the last time Peter Henneburry ever talked to his best friend.

Cecil, 39, and Andre, 26, did go out the next morning. They hauled their lobster pots early in the morning using the old boat, and then returned to port around 10:00 A.M. The weather was nearly perfect. Seas were calm and there was a very slight westerly wind of five knots. Sometime around noon the brothers decided to take advantage of the excellent weather and after lunch, headed out in their brand-spanking-new 21-foot open speedboat to haul a fleet of lumpfish nets in an area known locally as the Western Grounds. A fisherman in the area saw the Strickland brothers hauling their nets around three-thirty that afternoon with no indication of any trouble.

When darkness fell and the brothers had not returned home, their families became worried and a search was started around nine o'clock. Peter Henneburry was one of the first people to join the search, but he said a dense fog had rolled in with the darkness and there was no sign of the boat or the missing brothers. At daybreak the next morning, members of the local fire department conducted an ATV (all terrain vehicle) shoreline search, but still there was no sign of anything. Meanwhile, some fishermen hauled the fish nets set by the missing men the day before and discovered the first concrete sign that something had gone terribly wrong. A cap, owned by Andre Strickland, was found snagged in a net. A short while later, a RCMP Boston Whaler found the boat overturned several miles from where it was last seen. There was no sign of Andre or Cecil.

After searching for another day, the Canadian Coast Guard Search and Rescue effort ceased and the case was handed over to the RCMP as a missing persons case. The RCMP continued their efforts as they conducted remote-controlled underwater camera searches, but still nothing was found.

On June 7, 1988, 25 days after the incident, the body of Andre Strickland was found floating in Fairhaven Harbour, approximately 120 miles northeast of the Western Grounds near Allan's Island. There has never been a trace of Cecil Strickland.

What happened is still a mystery.

Because of the ideal weather conditions at the time of the loss, investigators can't even offer a probable scenario. Both men were experienced fishermen. Besides fishing from their open speedboat, Cecil and Andre also fished on board a small longliner together with other brothers. Although the fibreglass speedboat was brand new, it was one of many boats made from the same mould and there had never been a report of any stability problems with any of them. The throttle of the new 60-horsepower outboard motor was on "stop" and the gear lever was in the "neutral" position, indicating the motor was not running at the time of the accident. Ropes or nets had not fouled the propeller and the fuel tank was still attached to the motor. Their lump nets were located in deep water, so it's not likely they struck rocks.

But there was something that has caused some people to wonder. The boat was not damaged, but there was a reddish-colour scrape mark approximately three inches wide by seven or eight inches long on the port side of the hull, just aft of the stem near the waterline. What could have caused such a bright mark on a brand new boat on her maiden voyage?

It is possible that the scrape had nothing to do with the capsizing. It's anyone's guess. Local lore has theories ranging from a possible collision, a marine version of hit and run, to a collision with a log or some other floating debris, to striking or being struck by something else, either accidentally or deliberately. It could be any one of a hundred things, but sadly, only one thing is for sure; Friday, May 13, 1988 was the *final voyage* for brothers Cecil and Andre Strickland.

Algermon Trimm
"I'm just happy to see my grandchildren grow"

For many fishermen their final fishing voyage silences them forever. Although a horrible accident robbed him of the ability to ever fish again, Algermon Trimm is alive to tell the story of his last trip.

The 43-year-old inshore draggerman from English Point, Forteau in Labrador was fishing out of Cow Head on Newfoundland's west coast in the spring of 1980. Things were going well for the first few days of the spring fishery – cod were plentiful and Algermon and his crew were in good spirits.

Having spent most of his working life in the construction business and constantly working away from home, Algermon was feeling good about his decision to quit that life in 1978 and to come home and start a new life as a fisherman.

Monday, May 26, 1980, was a perfect spring day on the west coast. Skies were clear and winds were light. Algermon, along with his 17-year-old son, Gaius, Algermon's brother-in-law Claude Normore, and Claude's son Winston, left Cow Head about five o'clock that morning to haul six fleets of cod nets. The nets were set about 25 miles offshore, a two-and-a-half-hour steam in their 53-foot vessel, *Sea Queen.*

The four men fished all morning with only a break for lunch. At 2:15 P.M., the four were in their usual positions and started hauling the last fleet of 10 nets. Algermon was working the gurdy (winch),

Gaius was behind his father, cleaning the fish from the nets, while Claude and Winston were pulling back the nets in the stern of the vessel, getting them ready to set again.

No one saw exactly what happened, but somehow Algermon got caught in the net and got pulled around the gurdy. Before Gaius could run to cut the power to the winch, his father was wrapped around it so far that his body became jammed against a steel pipe that was bolted to the wheelhouse. Powerful enough to winch more than a ton of nets, the hydraulic-powered gurdy hardly slowed as Algermon's head was pulled, twisted and forced back over his shoulder against the three-foot steel pipe. Although only a few seconds had elapsed before Gaius grabbed the power switch, it was nearly too late; his father's neck was already severely broken.

Gaius frantically chopped the nets, while Claude and Winston untangled Algermon from the twine as they placed his unconscious body on the fishhold hatch cover. Gaius held his dad for the next two and a half hours while Claude piloted the vessel to port. Claude had radioed from the vessel while steaming to port and an ambulance met them at the wharf. Algermon was then rushed to the nearest cottage hospital in Woody Point, Bonne Bay.

Except for seeing daylight for a few seconds while lying on the hatch and thinking that he couldn't move his arms or legs, Algermon didn't regain consciousness for five days. The next thing he remembers is opening his eyes and seeing something white.

"It was doctors, the nurse told me afterwards, two doctors in white." That was the first couple of seconds in what would become a long journey to only partial recovery.

"They told me a few days later that I would never walk again," he said.

With his neck supported by a steel plate fastened by five bolts, Algermon Trimm spent the next 14 months in hospital in St. John's. Although, still a teenager

Algermon Trimm

at the time, Algermon's son Gaius took over as skipper of the *Sea Queen* and continued to fish for the next four years.

"I'm proud of him," Algermon says, smiling. "It wasn't easy but he had a lot of courage."

Courage seems to run in the family. Life is still not without pain and disappointment for Algermon Trimm and his family, but he's philosophical about it.

"I'm just happy to have been given the chance to see my children grow, and now I have five grandchildren that I would never have known if the worst had happened that day."

It may have been his last fishing trip, but May 26, 1980 was not to be Algermon Trimm's *final voyage*.

Waterspout Takes Eight
Nova Scotia Fishermen

No one knows exactly what happened to the longliner *Johnny and Sisters II* in early December 1989. Not one of the eight crew members survived to tell the tale. After a thorough examination of the available information, the best that investigators can do is make an educated guess. But whatever caused the loss must have been sudden and it must have been powerful.

The *Johnny and Sisters II* was well known to Newfoundlanders on the southern shore of the Avalon Peninsula. The fishing vessel out of Louisbourg, Nova Scotia, frequently landed in ports like Cape Broyle and Trepassey during fishing trips to the Grand Banks. During the first week of December in 1989, the *Johnny and Sisters II* was fishing on the Banks approximately 160 miles south of Newfoundland. The 19-metre longliner was last heard from around suppertime on December 3, 1989.

About seven o'clock that evening a crew member from the *Johnny and Sisters II* contacted the *7 Girls*, a 24-metre steel-hulled longliner fishing nearby. He announced their intention to depart the Grand Banks and head for two days of fishing on the Banquereau Bank.

That was the last-known radio communication from the ill-fated vessel.

There may have been one more radio contact from the *Johnny and Sisters II* but no one can be sure. Sometime between 7:00 A.M.

and eight o'clock the next morning, December 4, the skipper of another vessel in the area heard someone on the VHF radio exclaim "What!" Although he heard just that one single word, the skipper of the *Flying Dart* said he was reasonably confident he recognized the voice of Harry Thorburn, the 41-year-old captain of the *Johnny and Sisters II*.

Because there were no survivors, investigators could only piece together information supplied by others who were fishing in the area at the same time. One thing is certain; the weather in the area was bad, very bad. Gale warnings were in effect for the first 11 days of December in 1989. On December 7 and 8, high winds and heavy seas in the Gulf of St. Lawrence overwhelmed two cargo vessels. All 39 crew members of the *Capitaine Torres* and *Johanna B* were lost. At first, investigators thought the *Johnny and Sisters II* was also lost in that storm but, after reviewing the evidence, they concluded the fishing vessel from Louisburg, Nova Scotia was probably lost several days earlier, when it was suddenly overcome by extreme weather conditions.

The crew of the *7 Girls* reported that a severe storm struck the area on the morning of December 4, but they said it only lasted a short while. Those on board described it as the worst weather they had ever experienced at sea, with winds estimated, at times, at 100 knots or more.

But the extremely high winds were not the worst of it. Accompanying the winds were heavy rain and lightning and the most frightening thing of all was the occurrence of what was described as a "waterspout."

Waterspout Illlustration by Ian Williams.

Waterspouts are essentially a marine version of land-based tornadoes. They are rarely more than 200 metres wide at sea level and move fairly slowly. Like tornadoes, waterspouts have an average life span of about eight or nine minutes and several may occur in the same area at the same time. Waterspouts rotate rapidly above the ocean surface, with the wind following a circular path. The violent winds almost always lead to turbulent seas as the spout passes by.

The master of the *7 Girls* said a turning wall, or funnel of water, estimated to be 60 feet high, struck his vessel around 9:30 A.M. on December 4. The extreme winds and violent seas heeled his steel vessel on her beam ends, turning her around in circles several times.

One crew member said the vessel was going around like a spintop. Another described a feeling of being pulled to the deck by some unknown intense pressure, and then experiencing a sensation similar to a car going over a steep hill at high speed and then suddenly dropping. One wave smashed a fibreglass-sheathed plywood door to pieces and water flooded the fish slaughterhouse. The *7 Girls* sustained heavy water damage during that period, but not enough to disable her.

About an hour later, the skipper of another vessel, about 25 miles to the southeast, reported the same strange weather phenomenon had passed by his position. That vessel was not in the direct path of the spout.

After the system passed by and things returned to some degree of normalcy, the skipper of the *7 Girls* tried to contact the *Johnny and Sisters II*.

There was no response.

At 9:45 A.M. on December 9, the Nova Scotia clam dragger *Scotian Surf* sighted a body in an orange immersion suit in position 44.29.9 N – 52.36.0 W. It was the body of Paul Douglas Boutet, a 25-year-old crewman from the *Johnny and Sisters II*.

Although some debris was recovered, there was no sign of the vessel and nothing to indicate what had happened. One life raft was also recovered but there was no indication that anyone had ever used it.

There is no single scenario that might explain what happened to the *Johnny and Sisters II*. No one even knows when she was lost, but the evidence strongly suggests the longliner must have been overwhelmed by weather conditions that were both sudden and extreme. There was no distress call heard and there were no flares or rockets spotted. There was only one life raft recovered, indicating the crew may have only had time to release that one, and when the body of Paul Boutet was found, he was wearing only undershorts inside his immersion suit and the suit was filled with water. That indicates he didn't have time to dress in warm clothes and that the vessel may have already been awash when he put the suit on.

Transport Canada investigators believe the weather condition that caused the loss was more than likely a waterspout.

The marine casualty report states:

From the evidence that the 45 minutes or so after passing the 7 Girls, the waterspout(s) reached the area of another vessel which was 25 miles to the southeast, it could be calculated the meteorological system generating the spout(s) was moving at the rate of about 30 knots. It is conceivable then that, having struck the 7 Girls at 0930, the spout(s) could have been some 60-70 miles to the west of that vessel between 0700-0730. That would have placed the Johnny and Sisters II *(in that position) at about the time the lone word "What!" was heard by the* Flying Dart *and could perhaps account for the inflection of exclamation on that single word, had it been spoken by Mr. Thorburn. The casualty to the* Johnny and Sisters II *may have occurred at that time.*

Whatever the cause, the outcome is certain; the *Johnny and Sisters II* ended its *final voyage* in early December 1989.

Haunting Message Tells Fate of Lost Sealers

Saturday, April 7, 1917, was a typical early spring day on Fogo Island. A full week of northeasterly winds had packed heavy Arctic ice solidly against the shoreline on most of Newfoundland's northeast coast. The ice extended offshore as far as one could see, making conditions ideal for Fogo Island sealers. After a long harsh winter, a meal of flippers and seal meat would be a welcome adornment to the dinner tables in homes all around the island.

By six-thirty Saturday morning, dozens of men had congregated at various headlands where ice had jammed tightly onshore. With both the ice and shoreline covered in snow 12 to 15 inches deep, sealers could simply continue walking and hardly know whether they were on land or on the ice floes.

Brothers Joseph, Stephen and Walter Jacobs, along with their friend, Francis Pomroy, all from the south side of Joe Batt's Arm, were among the first out. Not far behind were William and Hubert Freake from the north side of Joe Batt's Arm.

Meanwhile, 21-year-old Patrick (Paddy) Higgins and several companions decided to leave from Brooks Point that morning. Skipper Nath Brett, the lighthouse keeper at Brooks Point, kept an eye on Paddy and his friends as they ploughed through knee-deep snow looking for the first sign of seals. Meanwhile, another friend, John Adams, was also keeping a watch on the sealers. John had intended to join his friends on the ice, but instead, he decided to check

135

on his two cows that had gone astray and wandered inland to the top of a hill near Brooks Point. Paddy and his friends had not gone far when they heard John Adams shouting at the top of his voice.

"Come back! Come in!" he called. "The fog is comin' in and the wind is checkin' off Southard! Come back!"

Although Paddy and his friends couldn't immediately see the conditions that John was describing, they knew that he had a good view from the top of the hill and they thought they had better heed his advice. By the time the men had discussed their options, fog had already started rolling in and the southerly wind that John had warned them was coming had already started moving the tightly packed ice pans apart.

Paddy Higgins always carried a compass with him and this would be one day when it came in handy. Based on the direction the ice was moving, the men decided to set a course for Round Point. That's where they figured they'd have the best chance to get ashore given the current conditions. Getting back to shore was going to be a challenge. The ice pans that just an hour before had been pushed solidly together by winds and tides were now being pushed apart by winds and tides flowing in the opposite direction. Tying a safety rope around their chests, the men would run and jump from one ice pan to another, sometimes landing in waist-deep wet slush ice. They ran and jumped until finally, all of them made it safely ashore at Big Greeps Cove.

"There was seven of us on one pan once. I jumped, but I only filled one of me boots," Paddy would laughingly boast later.

Shortly after Paddy and friends made it back home that morning, Steve Freake came by looking for men to help search for the three Jacobs brothers and their friends. Steve was concerned that the missing men might be unable to reach land because the ice had been pushed too far offshore. Without hesitation, Paddy and two other men were in Steve's punt headed, once again, to the offshore ice floes.

"We poked out through the ice until we came to a big island of ice. The fog was real thick and I could tell the ice was runnin' up (in a northerly direction)," Paddy said. Following in the wake of the fast-moving ice, the four rescuers rowed until they heard the sound of men calling. At one point the fog lifted long enough for Paddy to see what appeared to be several men in the distance slowly walking in the direction of Brooks Point. From there came the sound of guns firing. Shooting guns as a guide for stranded hunters was common practice in those days.

Sadly, weather conditions soon worsened and skipper Steve had to make a tough decision. With fog thickening and ice conditions becoming dangerous to their own safety, Steve knew he had to consider the well-being of the three men in the little boat with him. "We got to turn this punt around boys. We're going up on the rocks and we'll be jammed if we don't turn her around now," he said.

According to Paddy, Steve's decision was just in time. After battling with tightly packed ice pans moving quickly in heavy tides, Paddy said they had a hard time finding what he described as "a black vein of ice," meaning navigable waters despite being covered by thin ice and snow. It appears darker on the surface than the rest of the pans. Fortunately, they did find that black vein of ice, eventually making it to open water and then back once again to Brooks Point.

Out on the ice floes, the stranded men trudged slowly onwards toward the sound of gunfire until the noise and their hopes faded in the distance. With a widening gulf of water and loose ice floes between them and land, the only thing they could hope for was a sudden change of wind to drive the ice back towards land.

The wind didn't change.

Walter, Stephen and Joseph Jacobs, along with Francis Pomroy and William and Hubert Freak were never seen again. The only hint of their cruel fate surfaced two months later. In early June, near Morton's Harbour, a fisherman picked up the sealing gaff belonging to one of the Jacobs brothers. A message was inscribed on the wooden handle of the gaff. The message read: "April 11 – lying down to die."

The gaff was presented to Thomas and Mary Jacobs in memory of their only sons. Today, the gaff is located in the Anglican Church in Joe Batt's Arm as a memorial to the six men who made their *final voyage* in April 1917.

Thanks to Cyril Burke for providing the details for this story. Cyril recorded an interview with Paddy Higgins when the late Mr. Higgins was 90.

Like Dreaming in Slow Motion

"A nicer man you couldn't find anywhere on earth."

That's how Ron Dobbin remembers a longtime friend Charlie Parrot from O'Donnells, St. Mary's Bay. The two men were not only close friends, but they also worked together as well. Charlie, the younger of the two, was a crew member on Ron's longliner, *Darrell and Denise*.

During the first week of May in 1988, the *Darrell and Denise* had spent several days fishing herring near Long Harbour, Placentia Bay. Fishing had been good so Ron, owner and skipper of the 52-foot longliner, decided to go home to St. Mary's Bay for the weekend. On Friday evening, May 6, the two friends got together at Charlie's house for a beer and made plans for Saturday. The forecast called for cool but fine weather that weekend, so the two fishermen decided to set several trap moorings on Saturday afternoon. Charlie, known as hard worker, said he would haul his lobster traps early in the morning while Ron prepared the moorings. "I'll have some lobsters for your Mother's Day dinner on Sunday, my dear," Charlie called to Bride Parrott, his wife and mother of their three daughters.

After Ron left to return to his house that evening, Charlie and Bride sat at the kitchen table and discussed the plans for the next day. Bride always wanted to know when she should expect her husband home, especially when he fished alone; otherwise she'd start worrying within minutes after he'd left the wharf. Ordinarily, their daughter Charleen would have gone lobster fishing with her 36-year-old father that morning, but she was participating in a weekend basketball tournament in St. John's and had to take a rain check on this trip. Although she was only 12 years old, Charleen never missed an opportunity to get out in a boat with her dad.

Knowing Bride's tendency to worry excessively, Charlie carefully explained to his wife that if he could get away from the harbour about 6:30 A.M., he would haul the pots located near O'Donnell's Head, about a mile and a half from the wharf. And then, if everything went well, Charlie reckoned that he would probably be back home again by nine o'clock – in time for breakfast.

Saturday morning dawned, a fine spring day. There was a slight southerly breeze with a forecast temperature high of seven degrees Celsius. With only a small ripple on the water to contend with, Charlie was comfortably hauling his first lobster pot within minutes of his planned start time of 6:45 A.M.

Back in O'Donnells, Ron Dobbin was busy in his fishing shed preparing the moorings that he planned to set with Charlie later that day. Bride Parrott was working at routine Saturday morning chores around the house, occasionally glancing out the window, keeping a close eye on the ocean, making sure there was nothing to worry about. Despite nearly ideal weather conditions, Bride did worry though. When there was no sign of Charlie at 8:45 A.M., she called a neighbour to see if he was going down to the harbour anytime soon. Bride said she was worried and wanted to go down to the wharf to see if she could spot Charlie coming in the bay. Her neighbour humorously chided Bride to stop worrying so much, pointing out that Charlie even said he wouldn't be in until nine o'clock that morning.

Despite his wife's sense of impending trouble, Charlie Parrott was punctual as usual. Just before 9:00 A.M., the flat-bottomed boat was nearing the wharf in O'Donnells. Standing in the stern with one hand on the handle of the outboard motor, Charlie was guiding the small boat toward the wharf when suddenly, something went wrong. The boat sheared hard to port, toppling Charlie over the stern, into the ocean.

Several men who had congregated on the wharf for a chat that morning had been watching as Charlie approached the dock, but suddenly they felt like they were dreaming in slow motion as they stared at the water in shocked amazement. Almost in the blink of an eye, the only thing they could see was Charlie's empty boat motoring around in circles, just 50 feet from the wharf. There was no sign of the healthy young man they would have expected to see swimming, perhaps even laughing at himself for falling overboard.

Charlie was not laughing and he was not swimming.

Charlie was nowhere in sight.

Giving themselves a mental shake, the men knew they had to do something to try and save Charlie, and they knew they had to do it quickly. Two of the men alerted Felix Dobbin, who was working on board his fishing vessel tied to the wharf. Jumping aboard the boat, two of the men helped Felix quickly cut the lashings from a dory that was secured on the deck of the longliner. Although the men got the rescue boat into the water as fast as they could, it was too late.

Charlie Parrot.

Charlie Parrott's lifeless body was lying on the bottom in less than 20 feet of water.

No one knows what happened that Saturday morning. Even today, friends and relatives still shake their heads in wonderment when they discuss the accident. Charlie was in excellent condition. Ron Dobbin remembers many times when he and Charlie would go rabbit hunting.

"I'd have to sit down and take a spell sometimes but he'd walk on and on and finally come back and poke fun at me for being like an old man or 'over the hill' as he would say," Ron says with a chuckle.

Others remember Charlie as a strong swimmer who would sometimes dive in the ocean from the side a fishing boat and surface on the opposite side. But when Charlie fell overboard that morning, it appears that he could not move.

The question is: Why?

There was no evidence that he'd had a heart attack or suffered a seizure. Neither was there an indication that he fainted or struck his head during the fall. On the other hand, no one is certain whether doctors checked to determine if anything like that had happened. An autopsy cited drowning as the cause of death. But everyone who knew Charlie says that something strange happened. They all agree that when Charlie hit the water, he was incapacitated for some reason – otherwise, they say, Charlie would have easily survived a simple fall overboard.

The only thing they know for sure is that on Saturday, May 7, 1988, 36-year-old Charlie Parrot made his *final voyage*.

It Sounded Like Waves Crashing on the Rocks
The Loss of the *Straits Pride II*

It was supposed to be the last fishing trip before Christmas 1990 for the crew of the *Straits Pride II*, but little did they know that for three of them it would be their final voyage. Winter weather in mid-December kept the 65-foot wooden-hulled longliner secured in St. John's Harbour for a few days, where they took advantage of the time to replace a troublesome radio telephone. At 4:00 A.M. on December 15, 1990, Captain Archie Bond from Burnt Islands on the southwest coast of Newfoundland and his crew of five men left St. John's on a 16-hour trip to the fishing grounds east of St. John's. With Captain Bond were: his brother Russell, also from Burnt Islands; his cousin Max Purchase, from La Poile; Ross King from Isle aux Morts; Rob McDonald from Burnt Islands, and Harold Martin from Marystown.

The trip went well and by ten o'clock the next morning, December 16, the crew had set their otter trawl and began dragging for fish. During the second tow just after noon, a fisheries inspector from DFO boarded the *Straits Pride II*. After he completed the routine inspection, the officer prepared to go back and board the patrol vessel *Cape Roger*, but paused to inform the skipper of the *Straits Pride II* of a storm warning in the forecast. Captain Bond replied that fishing seemed to be good and his trip quota of nearly 100,000 pounds would likely be filled later that same day, and that in all probability, they would be back in port before the storm reached the area.

The crew continued to fish in good weather conditions until after midnight, when their quota was reached. At 1:30 A.M. the *Straits Pride II* departed the fishing grounds and headed for St. John's with a full load of fish. Five hours later, at 6:30 A.M., the inshore dragger made VHF radio contact with the vessel's owner that they were 92 miles from port and steaming at seven knots. The skipper indicated that winds and seas were increasing but that all was well. Eight hours later the owner was advised that the *Straits Pride II* was only 44 miles from St. John's and that weather conditions were worsening, with 35- to 45-knot southeast winds and high seas. The vessel was retaining seas on deck, although everything seemed to be fine.

Fifteen minutes after that call, the port paravane (a stabilizing device lowered from a boom into the water to reduce vessel roll) snapped and sank. Without the port stabilizer the vessel listed slightly to starboard, however the rough sea conditions were considered too dangerous for the men to go on deck to try and bring up the starboard paravane to provide the desired balance. There was no release mechanism in the wheelhouse to jettison the stabilizer, so the skipper decided another tactic. He decided to shut off the engine fuel supply from the tank on the port side, which was 90 per cent full, and use fuel from the starboard tank, which was about 30 per cent full. That might have helped, but the vessel had already started to retain a lot of water on deck, and the starboard list was becoming much greater. Various manoeuvres, including reducing speed, running with the wind and running directly *into* the wind proved unable to clear seas from the deck. A check below deck indicated there was no significant amount of water in the bilge, but one of the crew members noticed water in the fishhold where the fish was stowed. Water on top of the fish caused deep concern, because wet fish easily shifts positions, which in turn can lead to further imbalance and greater listing. Pumps were activated, but for some reason the water in the fishhold was not draining to the pump suction.

Facing waves between 10 and 15 feet and winds of 45 knots, the skipper ordered all hands to don their life jackets, as he called the Coast Guard radio station in St. John's requesting an escort for the *Straits Pride II*. It was 3:40 P.M. Seven minutes later the Coast Guard dispatched Search and Rescue Vessel *Sir Wilfred Grenfell*, but it was too late for an escort. A few minutes after that, at 4:04 P.M., in what would be the final communication from the *Straits Pride II*, the skipper radioed that it was already necessary to abandon ship.

Abandonment did not go well. The list had increased to such an extent the starboard rail was totally immersed, making it almost impossible for the crew to launch the aluminum lifeboat or the inflatable life raft. Rob McDonald and Harold Martin were on the roof of the wheelhouse frantically trying to release the life raft, but before they could get the raft properly positioned, a huge wave heeled the vessel even farther and the two men were nearly tossed into the ocean. They managed to free the life raft and since it appeared inevitable that they were going to be thrown overboard any minute, they decided to jump. They missed the raft but landed near enough to climb aboard.

Meanwhile, Ross, who was way back on the stern of the vessel, saw what his friends had done and decided they made the right decision. Since he was being tossed around by the seas, he figured he would follow the lead of his shipmates, so he jumped and started to swim toward the raft. He made it, and with Rob and Harold's help, he managed to climb on board the little rubber life raft too.

No one knows why Archie, Russell and Max didn't jump overboard along with the other three men. Ross King said he observed them waiting, perhaps weighing their options, or as Ross remembers, looking like they were in a frozen state, not sure of the best thing to do. Circumstances soon decided their fate. The vessel lurched one last time, rolling out on her beam ends, and the *Straits Pride II* started to rapidly submerge, throwing the remaining three men into the ocean.

Attempts to paddle the life raft toward the men in the water proved futile. Paddling as furiously as they could, the raft would go 10 feet ahead, only to be swept back 30 feet by seas and winds. Even as Ross and Rob paddled, trying to reach the men in the water, the skipper, Archie Bond, was shouting at them to keep away from the nearly submerged *Straits Pride II*. That was the last they heard from Archie or the others. A few minutes later their life raft was drifting out of sight as the *Straits Pride II* finally plowed under the surface, stern first.

Surviving the nine hours of darkness that it took for the *Grenfell* to arrive is still surreal to the three men in the life raft. Harold suffered from hypothermia and became delusional, but Ross and Rob managed to keep him going by taking off his boots and putting his feet inside their clothing to keep him warm. As unlikely as it would seem, they even joked. Ross remembers that when they first saw the bright searchlights from the *Grenfell* about 1:00 A.M., he joked to Harold they were about to be run over by a tractor-trailer.

"It was trying to keep Harold's spirits up," he remembers.

147

There were times though when it was no joking matter. Rough seas nearly capsized the little raft several times.

"You could hear them coming," Ross said. "It sounded like waves crashing on the rocks, it was that loud." And when the waves hit, they were practically submerged as the weight of the water crushed them to the floor of the raft. Whether it looked like lights from a tractor-trailer or not didn't matter – the searchlights from the *Grenfell* was the prettiest sight they had ever seen. Ross King, Rob McDonald and Harold Martin were rescued with minor injuries.

For the *Straits Pride II*, Captain Archie Bond, his brother, Russell, and their cousin, Max Purchase, this was their *final voyage*.

Even His Funeral Had to Wait

Nothing but old age could kill Jim Green. And even then he didn't go peacefully.

Even time had to wait for the fisherman from Witless Bay. Green was nearly 98 years old when he died in 1930.

"He was a big man – over six feet tall and well built," says Steve Green, looking at a picture of his grandfather in a battered old wooden frame. The survivor of several shipwrecks, smallpox, diphtheria and even "black fever" in South America, Jim Green was known as a "hard ticket."

Jim Green's first close call came when he was just 24. One of 26 crew members on a schooner called *The Hammer,* Jim was heading for Cape Broyle when a snowstorm struck on Monday evening, March 2, 1857. Sometime between 11:00 P.M. and midnight, Captain Tom Carew brought *The Hammer* around Brigus Head, the place he most worried about. After rounding the headland, thinking he was out of danger, Captain Carew misjudged his position and stayed too close to shore. When he realized he was in troubled waters, the captain let go the mainsail and dropped anchor but it was too late. *The Hammer* was holed by a sunker (sunken rock) and quickly filled with water. Twenty-four of the crew took to the lifeboats but the captain stayed on board. Young Jim Green took one look at the icy seas mercilessly pounding the small lifeboats, decided to stay on board with the captain and prepared to go down with the ship.

Jim made the right decision. As *The Hammer* sank lower into the ocean, the captain and the young crewman climbed the foremast until they could go no farther. As seas and ice pounded the lifeboats, there was nothing the two men could do but watch as all 24 of their shipmates were swamped and died just feet from the cliffs of Herring Cove.

For 12 hours, Jim Green and Tom Carew clung to the frozen mast and rigging of *The Hammer* before being sighted and rescued by Thomas Battcock around noon on March 3. After enduring a night and morning of unimaginable misery and suffering, Jim was taken to Cape Broyle where he was given dry clothes and a place to sleep. Undaunted by his adventure, the young Jim Green decided to walk home to Witless Bay the next day, a distance of nearly 20 miles.

A few years later, Jim was in South America picking up a load of cotton. While there, he was stricken with what he described as "black fever." Unconscious for three days, Jim remembered waking up confused and not knowing where he was. In a conversation with Sir Michael Cashin, a long-time friend, he described that experience.

"There was a 'darky' doctor standing alongside me and I heard him say 'this poor man is dying.' But I knew I was not dying, and in two weeks I was back to my work."

A well-travelled man, Jim Green left Liverpool, England one winter on a trip across the Atlantic to Newfoundland. The trip would normally have taken just a few weeks but rough seas and high winds blew them off course. It took two months before they finally made it to port. "We lost all moveables and one man was washed overboard too," he said in an interview, not bothering to explain whether the man was rescued or had died.

Once, while crossing Trinity Bay, Jim was knocked overboard by a swinging boom. As if being struck overboard wasn't enough misery, Jim was trying to swim back to his schooner when he was struck and run over by another schooner. In their haste to turn around, some of the ship's crew apparently fouled the sails and it took an hour before they could reach him. It would have taken his schooner much longer than that to rescue him, but Jim was a strong swimmer and had almost caught up to the vessel by the time they had things straightened out.

Jim Green's swimming abilities were tested on another occasion when he was caplin fishing out of Petty Harbour. Rough seas washed him and two shipmates overboard. He describes that day as "the time I had to do my best swimming." Neither of his two shipmates could swim and Jim was their only hope of surviving. Grabbing both men by their coat collars, he held on and kicked his feet, keeping all three afloat until they were finally rescued nearly an hour later.

Fisherman Patrick Lachlan was also thankful that his friend Jim was a strong swimmer. Fishing from the schooner *Eleanor Davis*, Patrick was washed overboard in heavy seas on the Flemish Cap, approximately 300 miles east of St. John's. Without a moment's hesitation, Jim quickly tied one end of a rope to the ship and the other end around his waist and jumped into the ocean to save his friend.

A few minutes later, both men were safe on board their schooner.

Jim Green couldn't resist a challenge. As a group of men were waiting to go sealing one spring, he and William Cole were competing in a broad jump to pass time. The idea was to jump across a 20-foot-wide open-water lead in the harbour ice. "Jim loved telling that story," says his nephew. "I went back about ten feet (to run) and went clear to the other side. Captain Cole followed next. He went in the water about two feet short of going over it. He made a grand hole in the water! They all cheered me and called me 'Green, the smart man.'"

Jim Green used to laugh at most of his adventures and misadventures, but it was no laughing matter in the1860s when his wife and eight children became stricken with diphtheria. All nine of them died within two weeks. Green himself was diagnosed with diphtheria, but unlike the rest of his family, he survived.

Even then, Jim hadn't seen the end of family tragedy. Six years later, the big fisherman remarried and eventually had seven more children. Plagued by bad luck, diphtheria struck again and all seven children from his second marriage died. His second wife survived and the couple had one more child. Fred Green lived to be 80.

The only time Jim admitted to being scared was once when he was seal hunting from a large schooner. After working away from the ship on the ice all day, he and his sealing partner Jim Cashin were heading back to the ship when Jim Cashin collapsed. "The last words he said to me were 'Green, stand to my body.'" Green managed to get his friend to a nearby ship and 'stood by.' "I was so uneasy about the man's last words, I stuck to him until they held an inquest over

Steve Green with a picture of his grandfather Jim Green.

the body. The doctor pronounced that the heart left its berth before he died," Jim lamented.

Surviving against incredible odds, Jim Green surprisingly lived to a ripe old age. The mariner from Witless Bay died on September 19, 1930. He was 98.

Even after his death, Jim Green didn't seem to want to go quietly. In fact, he created one last fuss. Jim had purchased his own casket and brought it home two years before his death. When it came time to take him out, the casket wouldn't fit the door opening of the renovated house. Fittingly for the tough guy, it seems, pallbearers had no choice but to knock a window out of his house before taking Jim Green on his *final voyage*.

Beautiful Morning Comes to Tragic End

There's something about the beauty of an early spring morning on the western side of Placentia Bay that makes even night owls want to stay up till after sunrise. That's why Tom Keating and Harry Upshall from Baine Harbour on Newfoundland's Burin Peninsula didn't mind getting up before daylight on May 12, 1992.

Tom, aged 40, and his fishing partner, 45-year-old Harry, had watched hundreds of sunrises from their boat steaming to the fishing grounds. That morning, the two fishermen had their fuel and all other gear and equipment ready to head out even before the sun peeped over Cape St. Mary's in the east.

It was seasonally cool that Tuesday morning, with just a slight southerly breeze blowing into Placentia Bay. With such fair weather conditions, the experienced fishermen figured it was a good time to move their lobster pots from just off nearby Cross Island to Green Island, about six miles away. The lobster season was three weeks old and they wanted to make sure they followed the seasonal movements of the lobster to maximize their catch rate that spring.

By 6:00 A.M., Tom and Harry had hauled 30 pots. With the lobster pots secured neatly in the mid to bow section of the 20-foot speedboat, Tom started the outboard motor while Harry sat just behind the stack of wooden pots. The five-mile trip went smoothly. Approaching Green Island, Tom asked Harry what would be a good time and place to stop the boat and set the first few pots.

"Anytime you feel like it now, I think," Harry shouted, over the noise of the engine. As Harry climbed up over the stack of lobster pots to get a better look at their position, Tom cut the engine's power. That's when Harry saw that the bow section of the speedboat had filled with water. No one is certain what exactly caused the water buildup, but Harry thinks it might have had something to do with water splashing over the bow and bouncing off the pots, back into the boat.

"Also, I think the water might have holed up there because we had a lot of bags of lobster bait stowed up forward," Harry says. The bait bags functioned like sandbags and stemmed the flow of water to the back of the boat. Regardless of the cause of the water buildup, one thing is certain; when Tom cut the engine's power, the boat's slowing motion caused all the water to slosh to the bow and within seconds the loaded speedboat, and lobster pots, along with Harry and Tom were swamped.

It happened so fast that both men were stunned to find themselves treading water, looking for the boat that they had been sitting in just moments before.

"All I remember is that just as the front went under, I saw three life jackets floating towards me. They were stowed up front and when they floated up, they landed right in my hands," Harry recalls. A non-swimmer, Harry tucked one life jacket under his arm as he threw a second jacket to Tom. Although Tom could swim, he didn't try to put on the jacket either, opting instead to do the same as Harry and nipped it under one arm.

For a few moments it appeared that things would work out fine. Besides the good luck of having life jackets float to them, the boat suddenly surfaced a few feet away. Although the boat was bottom up, the two fishermen could at least get out of the cold water by climbing up on the overturned hull. With any luck the sun would keep them warm enough to last until a fishing boat came by and rescued them. Sitting on the boat, Tom and Harry scanned the waters of Placentia Bay looking for a sign of fellow fishermen who might be in the area tending lobster pots or hauling fish nets. They didn't have to wait long. About 7:30 A.M., a speedboat with two fishermen from

Red Harbour on board was speeding their way. *Perfect timing*, Harry and Tom thought, knowing the cold temperatures would soon cause them great discomfort and possibly hypothermia. Suddenly, their elation turned to despair. Although the boat was only 500 feet away, it continued to speed on by and out of sight. Later, Harry and Tom realized that the fishermen in the speedboat didn't see them because of the bright sunlight shining in their eyes.

Although the sun was providing some warmth, the near-freezing temperatures kept the men's soaked clothing from drying. By 8:00 A.M. the two fishermen were shivering uncontrollably. Tom said he found it warmer in the water, so he kicked his boots off and slid from the bottom of the boat into the ocean. Finding himself quickly tiring in the water Tom was aware of the symptoms of hypothermia and decided to climb back on the boat again. But the energy he had expended in doing so took a toll on him.

"By eight-thirty or so he was becoming delirious," Harry says. As the boat started to drift out the bay toward Jude Island, Harry tried to encourage his buddy to hang on for another while but sometime about ten o'clock that morning, Tom slipped from the boat for the last time.

As Jude Island loomed closer, Harry stood on the overturned hull of the speedboat and tried to keep the boat going in the right direction that would have it wash toward the beach. Just before noon, Harry crawled from the boat and waded ashore to the safety of Jude Island.

Despite being thrown overboard and spending more than four hours stranded on the bottom of a small boat shivering in near freezing weather, Harry was in surprisingly good condition. Even his baseball-style cap was still on his head, the same as when he left home that morning.

Harry had been on Jude Island many times and knew there were cabins on the western side of the four-mile-long island, but he also knew the cabins were nearly two hours walking distance from where he was standing. Afraid that he might slip on the icy rocks and fall in the water again, Harry decided not to walk along the shoreline. Climbing the cliffs and walking along a hillside path was a longer and a more difficult option, but he reasoned that it was safer.

Approximately an hour and a half later at 1:30 P.M., Harry approached a cabin near the beach. The door was locked but one smack with an axe that he found sitting on a nearby chopping block opened the door quite nicely. Inside the cabin, Harry was delighted to see a CB radio set that was in operating order. Picking up the microphone he placed a call to anyone who was listening, explaining that he was in trouble and needed help to look for Tom. Joy Kenway, wife of a fisherman in Baine Harbour, answered the call.

At 2:00 P.M., Harvey Reid from Baine Harbour clamoured up the hillside from the beach and joined Harry at the cabin. Although Harvey suggested that Harry should go home and rest, there was no way the fisherman could settle down until he searched for his fishing partner. The two men combed the waters of Placentia Bay till dark but there was no sign of Tom Keating. Sadly, that lobster trip on May 12, 1992 was Tom's *final voyage*.

The Rescuers
"Baptism by Fire" for Young
<u>Coast Guard Skipper</u>

It was baptism by fire!

That's how Captain Glen Mackey describes his first trip as commanding officer of the Fisheries Patrol vessel *Cape Roger* in 1996. On Thursday, October 15, his second day out, the 35-year-old captain received a call saying that the *Hamilton Banker* was requesting assistance. The vessel had lost power while fishing 105 miles offshore from St. John's. Although seas and winds were high, the *Hamilton Banker* was not in danger of sinking.

The *Cape Roger* carefully approached the disabled fishing vessel on her starboard quarter, and after successfully getting a towline on board, brought the ship and crew to port in St. John's.

The next day, the *Cape Roger* headed back to what everyone thought would be a routine patrol on the Grand Banks. Feeling good about his first accomplishment as commanding officer, Glen Mackey could never have prepared himself for his next call to duty.

On the afternoon of Thursday, October 23, the *Cape Roger* was a hundred miles outside Canada's 200-mile limit, riding out winds of 40 knots and seas three storeys high. At 12:35 P.M. they received word that the cargo ship *Vanessa* was sinking 150 miles farther out to sea. Without a moment's hesitation Captain Mackey altered course to ESE and ordered the engine room to run both engines full speed ahead. Luckily, the winds were on the stern of the patrol vessel, giving them extra speed.

"When we were riding down the crest of the waves we were doing as much as 20 knots," Captain Mackey said.

Before arriving on the scene, Captain Mackey learned the *Vanessa* had sunk and that nine of the 16-man crew were in life rafts. Sadly, the six remaining crew members were washed overboard in the heavy seas when they attempted to get aboard a raft.

With the news of men overboard, the mood aboard the *Cape Roger* became more sombre. Calculating the time since the men were swept into the ocean, Captain Mackey knew that even if he could locate the victims immediately upon arrival, he could be faced with dead bodies. Despite the warming influence of the Gulf Stream in the area, it was unlikely that anyone would survive more than 15 or 16 hours, even in survival suits.

Knowing it was going to be a long night, some of the crew tried to sleep, while the captain and officers were in constant contact with the Coast Guard Rescue Coordination Centre in Halifax preparing their rescue strategy.

At 7:40 P.M. two military aircraft had arrived on the scene and spotted a life raft with the nine crewmen in it. A large container vessel *Summer Wind* was nearing the area, but the 500-foot-long ship was not expected to be able to manoeuvre in the rough seas to get the men from the raft. Not willing to just sit and do nothing, the captain of the *Summer Wind* wanted to try a rescue effort. Amazingly, at

10:50 P.M., after several attempts, the nine men were plucked from the raft and pulled safely aboard the big cargo ship.

Darkness brought some improvement in weather conditions, but tensions on board the *Cape Roger* mounted as everyone realized their job now was the most gruesome task in a search and rescue mission. They were no longer looking for men in life rafts. Their job now was to locate and retrieve six men who had been in the water for many hours.

As the *Cape Roger* came closer to the scene, an ominous quiet descended over the vessel's crew when they first sighted night illumination devices being deployed from search-aircraft 20 miles away. Not being a Search and Rescue vessel, this would be the first time most of the crew of the fisheries patrol ship ever had to deal with this kind of mission.

As the *Cape Roger* approached the scene, Captain Mackey was designated by Rescue Headquarters as "On Scene Commander" of the four commercial vessels that had reached the area, including the *Summer Wind*, where the captain and eight crew members of the stricken ship were resting on board. The first job was to figure out a search plan to look for the victims. A device known as Self-Locating Datum Marker Buoys (DMBs) proved to be a valuable tool. Deployed by the aircraft, the DMBs measured drift on the ocean surface as well as surface temperatures. The data from the buoys is sent via satellite to the Rescue Coordination Centre.

Given the strong westerly winds that day, even experienced mariners would have been convinced the crew members had drifted several miles east of the location where they were washed overboard. The marker buoys told a different story. The DMB data showed strong ocean currents running in the opposite direction of the wind. As hard as it was to believe, the data indicated that the currents were fast enough to counter the effect of the high winds and were strong enough to carry a body upwind in a westerly direction instead of downwind in an easterly direction. Although this was the first time the DMBs had been used in an actual search and rescue incident, Captain Mackey trusted the technology and plotted his search pattern accordingly. His hunch turned out to be right.

At 3:35 A.M. a lookout on the *Cape Roger* spotted a person in a life jacket floating in the water. Glen Mackey's voice grows quieter

*Captain Glen Mackey and the crew of the **Cape Roger**.*

as he talks about seeing the man for the first time in the dead of night.

"Our men had spotlights directed on him and I could even see the whites of his eyes." The young captain didn't need a doctor to tell him the man was dead.

"There were no vital signs, so we knew what we were dealing with," he says.

For a few moments, a hush fell over the crew as they wondered what would face them next. The silence was broken only by the sound of the rescue team departing the *Cape Roger* in a Fast Rescue Craft (FRC) to retrieve the body. As the sky became illuminated again by the aircraft searching for the remaining five men, the first body was taken to the makeshift morgue in the helicopter hanger on the patrol vessel.

Just after daylight, the "lookout" spotted two persons, intertwined, floating in life jackets. The FRC was deployed and again it appeared they were dealing with two dead bodies, when suddenly they saw hands lifting from the water. Everyone on the FRC and the ship intuitively knew they were witnessing a miracle. Nineteen hours had gone by since the men were thrown into the ocean, and no one expected to see a survivor.

Although the man's pulse was so weak it was unreadable, the ship's medical team fought valiantly to save him. On the bridge, Captain Mackey's focus also changed from searching for bodies to searching for survivors.

Knowing the Search and Rescue (SAR) technicians in the aircraft were highly skilled and trained to handle situations like his crew were now facing, the captain asked if they would jump from the airplane and help treat the survivor. With no thought for their own safety, Master Corporal Darrell Cronin and Sergeant Mark Reeves jumped from the security of their aircraft into the rough seas, 450 miles from land. A few minutes later, they were pulled from the ocean by crew members from the *Cape Roger.*

While the technicians were preparing to jump, rescuers retrieved two more bodies.

This time, there were no vital signs of life.

At the same time, the survivor, who became known to the crew as Henry, was slowly improving. Handling him very gently, the crew cut off Henry's wet clothes and started the slow process of reviving his core body temperature. Because body heat from another person is an effective method of treatment for hypothermia, a fisheries officer on board the *Cape Roger* stripped to his underwear and got into the recovery capsule with Henry.

With Henry's recovery, morale greatly improved as the crew returned to the task of searching for the sixth and last person. At three o'clock Friday afternoon, a cargo ship spotted an empty life jacket. After identifying the jacket as belonging to the missing man, a search continued without success. Realizing it was impossible to survive in the ocean for that long without a life jacket, Captain Mackey again focused on saving Henry, the lone survivor. After getting the "all-clear" from the Rescue Coordination Centre, the *Cape Roger* altered course for St. John's.

The crewman known as Henry was taken to the Health Sciences Centre in St. John's. Amazingly, he was released in less than two hours, thanks to the valiant efforts of the *Cape Roger* and to the heroics of the SAR technicians.

Sadly though, there is a footnote to this story. One of the two SAR technicians who courageously helped in that rescue died tragically two years later. Master Corporal Darrell Cronin of Kelligrews, Newfoundland, aged 32, was killed when a Coast Guard Labrador helicopter crashed in Quebec on October 2, 1998.

A Whale Might Be to Blame
Uncle Ned Pittman's Final Voyage

Ned Pittman loved his life as a fisherman, especially on days like September 27, 1990.

The 60-year-old was up before sunrise that morning, getting ready to go squid jigging because he knew that as soon as the sun rose over White Bay, it was going to be a glorious day on the water. There was not enough wind to rustle up a single ripple on the ocean surface near Ned's home in Great Harbour Deep. "Uncle Ned," as he was known to many in his hometown, decided there was no reason to join the other three members of their fishing crew that Thursday morning. The cod fishing season had all but wrapped up and the only thing left to do on that front was to take in the Japanese-style cod trap from the berth that they had used that summer. Ned's sons Melvin and Nelson, along with Wilson Eldar, the fourth member of the Pittman crew, could get along without him on that job, so he decided to fish for squid by himself that morning. The crew needed squid to use as bait in their crab pots during the next several weeks and besides, if the squid jigging was really good, there was a market waiting to buy any surplus he might catch.

Just after sunrise Ned was speeding out the harbour in his 19-foot Neldo Marine speedboat. With his 60-horsepower Yamaha outboard motor near full open throttle, the fisherman would only be a few minutes reaching Northeast Arm, just beyond a point of land extending out from the mouth of Great Harbour Deep.

Meanwhile, things were going well for Melvin, Nelson and Wilson too. The three men were enjoying the summer-like weather and calm seas as they embarked on the trip to retrieve their cod trap located about 19 miles north of Great Harbour Deep, up the coastline toward Englee. Everything went as planned for the two Pittman brothers and Wilson Eldar. They hauled the cod trap and retrieved moorings and other parts of the gear and headed home early in the afternoon.

When they arrived home in Great Harbour Deep, the Pittman sons noticed that their father hadn't returned, but then they hadn't expected him back at that time either. Skipper Ned always took a lunch with him and usually stayed out as long as the fish were coming over the rails of the boat. Even when suppertime approached and Ned had still not yet arrived, no one worried. Ned Pittman was known to have fished till dark many evenings, especially on days when the weather was fine. But as darkness fell and there was still no sign on their father, Melvin and Nelson became concerned that something might have gone wrong. Because there was no wind or high seas to cause danger for their experienced fisherman father, the sons were not overly worried about his safety.

"We figured his engine had broke down and that's all there would be to it," says Nelson. Thinking they would simply have to steam out around the point and throw a line to their father and tow him and his speedboat back to port, the sons, along with Wilson, decided to take their longliner to do the job. The 50-foot vessel was equipped with radar and spotlights, equipment that would make it easier to locate Ned's boat in the dark.

As they steamed toward Northeast Arm, the three men chatted about where to search if Ned had moved from Northeast Arm during the day. They wondered if he might have finished squid jigging early, and decided to take advantage of the beautiful weather and spend a few hours berry picking somewhere on the hills near Great Harbour Deep. When they couldn't find any sign of the boat in the Arm, they knew their search area had suddenly widened considerably.

As the three men searched up and down the coastline in all the locations where they thought he might have tried squid jigging or had gone to pick berries, their mood grew more and more sombre. Some time around midnight they decided to go back home and contact the Coast Guard to ask for assistance.

At daybreak on Friday morning a dozen or more fishing boats from Great Harbour Deep, along with a Coast Guard vessel, were scouring the waters along more than 20 miles of coastline north and south of the small fishing village in White Bay. Despite ideal search conditions there was no sign of Ned or his speedboat. Hopes for a happy ending started to fade in the late afternoon when Kirby Ropson found Ned's fuel tank floating near the entrance to Great Harbour Deep, not far from Northeast Arm. Shortly afterwards, someone found an oar from his speedboat in the same vicinity.

The search continued for four days but nothing more was ever found. Memorial University officials even sent out technicians with a remote underwater camera, but still no trace of a speedboat or a body was seen.

The disappearance of Ned Pittman and his 19-foot speedboat is still shrouded in mystery. In the ideal weather conditions that day, it was extremely unlikely that the boat capsized or swamped. If the boat had struck a rock or even if a larger vessel had rammed into the smaller boat, there would have been wreckage. In the very unlikely event that the fibreglass speedboat sprang a leak and sank, it would have been located on the bottom near the vicinity where the tank and oar were recovered.

The Pittman family and others have ruled out all the usual causes in such a tragedy, leaving Ned's mysterious disappearance open to suggestion. Some people wondered about the possibly that a whale might be to blame. There had been earlier sightings of a humpback whale that apparently had been tangled in fishing gear – a long rope was seen trailing behind the animal as it travelled in the waters near Great Harbour Deep that week. Those people suggest that if the whale had been in the area feeding on squid it might have snagged Ned's fishing gear or anchor rope and dragged the speedboat down. Others wonder if another boat accidentally struck the small speedboat, causing it to suddenly sink.

People will probably speculate forever on what happened that day but the only thing certain is that Uncle Ned Pittman, one of Great Harbour Deep's best-known fisherman, made his *final voyage* on September 27, 1990.

A "Miraculous" Escape from a Watery Grave

Thirty-eight-year-old David Pretty is living proof that miracles do happen.

At least "miraculous" is the word most people use to explain how the fisherman from Dildo survived being dragged 70 feet to the bottom of the ocean, tangled in fishing ropes that were attached to a 250-pound anchor.

On June 20, 1998, David was setting his caplin trap in Marleys Cove near Dildo. After going ashore to attach his "shorefast" to run the main mooring for the trap, David got back in his 30-foot fishing boat ready to run his set-lines. His nephew, 17-year-old Adam Hollett, accompanied David on the trip to help his uncle set the trap.

After running out approximately 80 fathoms (480 feet) of rope, a knot in the line hooked in the end of a grapnel, flipping the anchor backwards over the side of the boat. Trouble was, David's foot got caught in the rope as it quickly uncoiled, pulled by the weight of the large anchor. Before he knew what had happened David went flying over the gunwale, landing backwards in the water.

Although it was only a second or two before he hit the water, David figured he was in big trouble. He knew the water was deep and he realized the anchor would pull him straight to the bottom. A moment later, his luck turned even worse when his other foot became tangled in a pile of rope that had been floating on the water.

"As soon as the rope tightened around my legs, I knew I was going to be gone for a long time so I

Illustration by David Pretty.

took a deep breath," he says calmly, looking out the window from his kitchen.

David Pretty is surprisingly clear on what happened next. He says it was only a few seconds before he found himself standing on the ocean floor facing the anchor, which was also standing upright on the bottom directly in front of him. A thousand thoughts flashed through his mind. He remembers thinking he would probably drown. That's when his thoughts flicked to his family. He wondered what would happen to his wife, Gaylia, his 17-year-old daughter, Diana and his seven-year-old son, Andrew.

Because it all happened so fast, David says he didn't have time to panic. He thinks that's why he is alive today.

"I remembered I had a knife in my pocket so I might be able to cut the rope from my legs. I also remember thinking not to struggle, because I might pull the rope tighter and I knew that would be the end of me."

But as luck would have it, David didn't need a knife, nor did he have to struggle to free his legs from the rope. David's head was filled with a roaring noise that he describes as sounding like an airplane taking off, but still he remained calm. He noticed that since the anchor came to rest on the bottom, the ropes had loosened around his legs. Reaching down, he slipped the ropes off, careful not to pull them the wrong way. As soon as he felt the rope fall away from him, David crouched down and gave himself a push and started his way back to the surface.

Although the trip back was much longer than it was going down, David remembers looking up and seeing light at the surface. That's when he knew he was going to make it.

David did make it, but just in the nick of time. Adam, waiting helplessly in the boat, says he thought his uncle had drowned.

"I remember thinking it was going to be a bad Father's Day the next day for his family," the young man says. Adam estimates his uncle had been under water for nearly two minutes. He remembers David gasping loudly and anxiously for air the moment he surfaced.

Today, David nonchalantly says, "There's no doubt I needed some air by then."

Although David's worst fears were over, he still had a concern. Admitting that he's "not much of a swimmer," David realized the boat was at least 50 feet away from where he surfaced. Somehow he managed to flounder his way to the boat and grabbed the gunwale. Happy that finally he could do something to help his uncle, Adam grabbed David and tried to pull him on board, but David, a big man, was too heavy to move. Weakened by the ordeal of the past several minutes, David was not able to help his nephew either but, again, his level-headedness prevailed. Kicking off his only remaining boot, David told Adam to let him rest for a couple of minutes.

"I had a hold of the gunwale and I knew I wasn't gonna let go but I needed time to catch my breath," he remembers. After several minutes resting in the water, he regained enough strength to hoist himself, with Adam's help, safely into the boat.

David spent the next 20 minutes sitting in the open boat, coughing and spitting up water that was, at times, mixed with blood. Although he was soaked, cold, shivering and weakened, he saw the hundreds of feet of his expensive ropes floating in the water and decided, with Adam's help, to continue the job they came out to do.

"I didn't feel there was anything major wrong so we took about an hour to finish the job before we left to go in," David says.

David didn't bother to see a doctor until the next day, and did so then only because so many people insisted that he must have severely damaged something or other. Everyone was convinced that water pressure at six storeys below sea level must have damaged his eardrums. Despite the well-meaning concerns of his friends, David knew he was all right, but Sunday morning he drove to St. John's to get checked out anyway.

The doctor told David just what he expected to hear. He was fine.

David says the experience didn't change his life in any way. His honest, philosophical take on the matter is simple.

"I would never do anything to hurt anyone before it happened and I'm still the same."

Although he takes the whole experience in stride, David Pretty doesn't take life for granted.

"I know that if I was in slightly deeper water or was under a few seconds longer, I wouldn't be here today," he says. He's grateful to have survived the ordeal. He's a careful fisherman and is fully aware that he came within, in his words, "a hair" of having made his *final voyage*.

Red Sky in Morning

George Bath took a long hard look at the bright red morning sky to the east of the Horse Islands on Saturday, April 14, 1962. The experienced fisherman and sealer could tell that, despite the nice sunrise, "weather" was on the way. There is something about the colour of the sky and the look of the water that makes people who live close to the land and sea understand intuitively when a storm is brewing. They can't explain it – they just know it. But despite threatening weather, the urge to go sealing was strong that Saturday morning. Malcolm Curtis had spread the word that he had seen a good patch of beaters (young harp seals) across the other side of White Bay on Friday, and George knew that it was time to gear up for the spring harvest. At least a dozen boats from the Island would be headed out bright and early that morning for their first harvest of the season.

Even though George was concerned about bad weather, his 19-year-old son Otis persistently tried to convince him that everything was going to be just fine. Otis was particularly eager to go, because a couple of young men from Wild Cove who had stayed overnight at the Bath household had already left for the ice.

Allan and Mark Small also heard the news that seals were coming in the bay, and left their homes in Wild Cove on Friday to take a first-hand look. Rather than steam all the way back home that evening, they spent the night with the Baths on the Horse Islands.

That way, they would be closer to the seal herd the next morning. Knowing that his friends had already gone, it would take more than the threat of a breeze of wind to discourage Otis Bath that morning.

"Well, all right then, but we might be sorry for this," his father warned, taking another glance at the ominous red sky.

Similar conversations took place in at least a dozen households on the Horse Islands that morning. Bob Bath and his friend Win (Edwin) Greenham noticed the sombre tell-tale sky too, but like George and Otis, it wasn't long before they had their minds made up to take a chance that it wouldn't get much worse. Horse Island men knew that a sudden change in wind direction could quickly move the ice and seals out to sea, taking with them the opportunity for a successful voyage. Famous for being amongst the best sealers in the country, not one man on the island wanted to miss a single minute sealing, even if it meant fighting a torturous, cold April wind.

Not wanting to be left out of the action, Bob Bath's 21-year-old son Purse grabbed his gun and joined his dad and Win Greenham as they headed for their small 21-foot open boat in the harbour. Another son, 16-year-old Austin, glumly watched his father and brother as they walked to the wharf. Austin also wanted to go on the trip but his father flatly refused to allow him on board the boat. "There is no rubber clothes for you and with a stiff breeze of wind, you're going to get soaking wet and freeze," Bob Bath explained to his son. An hour later, a heavy cloud cover turned the red sky to grey. By then, seven or eight boats were already on the way across White Bay, steaming towards the pack ice nearly 20 miles to the west.

Otis Bath remembers the trip across the bay as a quick one. "We passed Bob and Win and Purse by Western Harbour and I remember them pointing to the east and making motions that there might be a storm coming on," he says. Aided by an already stiff southeasterly breeze on their stern, Otis and George were at the edge of the ice in just over half the normal steam-time. Several boats had tied on to a large pan of ice as their skippers took a closer look at the storm clouds that suddenly appeared very menacing. It didn't take long for most of the older men to decide that the sensible thing to do was get back to the Horse Islands as fast as they could. It was obvious that this storm was going to be an ugly one. Some sealers had even decided to turn around before they got all the way across the bay. Others, including Allan and Mark Small had been at the ice edge for a while. In fact, their boat was nearly stuck in the moving ice, pushed by the winds and currents.

Although disappointed at the thought of losing a day sealing, George and Otis agreed that leaving was the right thing to do. By late morning, they were on their way home again knowing the trip back was going to take much longer than it took going the other way that morning. By noon the wind had strengthened to nearly 60 knots and seas were cresting at 25 to 30 feet high. Otis remembers the waves as "ugly, dark green and foaming at the top."

But things got worse.

As if ugly green roaring seas the height of a two-storey house were not enough to contend with, it started to snow. Whipped by the high easterly winds, the snow was blowing straight against their faces, making it nearly impossible to see the bow of the trap skiff.

"I remember my father, turning around with his back to the wind and snow and trying to keep her on course. He did a wonderful job figuring out the compass from the opposite direction and keeping her straight," Otis says with a smile, still proud of his father's expert seamanship. From the moment they left the ice, George and Otis had lost sight and contact with the other sealers, including Win Greenham and Bob and Purse Bath.

By the time Allan and Mark Small decided to head for shelter, it was too late. By then, both their trap skiff and their small speedboat were jammed between ice pans. They could lift the small speedboat and carry it across the ice to open water, but that wouldn't serve any purpose. To try and stay afloat in 30-foot seas in that little boat would have been impossible. They wouldn't have lasted 10 minutes and they knew it. They had only two options. They could stay on the constantly heaving ice with the boat and hope for the best, or they could try and walk four miles over the ice pans to shore.

It was a tough decision. Staying on the ice in a vicious snowstorm was tempting fate to the limit. What if the ice smashed their boat apart? What would happen if the wind suddenly changed or if the ice

Otis Bath.

176

moved offshore far out in the Atlantic Ocean? On the other hand, both men knew that picking their way over broken ice pans in blinding snow was extremely daunting at best. Blowing snow often covers the open water leads between ice pans, giving the appearance of solid ice. One misplaced step meant almost certain death if they fell into the frigid ocean. But, faced with the alternative of freezing to death on the ice, the two brothers decided that walking to land was their best option. After hauling their small speedboat up on a large ice pan in hopes that someone would find it, Allan and Mark Small knelt down and prayed.

While Allan and Mark Small prayed for guidance on what would undoubtedly be the most perilous journey of their lives, George and Otis Bath continued to battle their way through 30-foot seas, slowly inching toward home on the Horse Islands. Otis remembers one of the scariest moments on the trip came when his father tried to get to the front of the boat to retrieve something from a locker under the cuddy (bow). Leaving the relative comfort of the small engine house at the stern, George Bath got caught in a wave that washed over the open trapskiff.

"I remember looking at him as he was being washed around the gangboards, unable to control his movements at all," Otis says. Luckily, the elder Bath managed to hold on and made it back to the stern of the boat unhurt. Today, Otis remembers the moment by adding a tinge of humour.

"Father reminded me of a herring sloshing back and forth in water in the fishhold," he laughs.

Meanwhile, back on the ice floes, Allan and Mark trudged along the frozen pans toward land. Unable to see more than just feet ahead of them in the blinding snow, the brothers made sure to keep walking with the northerly wind blowing against the right side of their faces. That was the only way they could tell that they were heading in a westerly direction. As long as the wind didn't change, they knew that eventually they would reach land.

Their prayers for guidance were eventually answered. The two men made the four-mile trek across the ice without a serious incident. Although they were cold, wet and tired from fighting the winds and snow for hours, the sight of land gave the brothers renewed energy. When the snow squalls died down for several moments, Mark and Allan got a view of the shoreline and estimated they were about two miles down the coastline from Harbour Deep Point. Knowing there was no way they could make it over the mountains that towered in front of them, and then walk an additional five or six miles to the community of Harbour Deep, the men decided they had just one chance to find the shelter they needed to survive. There was a small lighthouse perched on Harbour Deep Point and, although it fell short in comparison to a five-star hotel, the little lighthouse looked like a mansion to Allan and Mark, considering their alternatives at the time.

Around the same time that the Small brothers made it to the lighthouse, Otis and George Bath caught a glimpse of the Horse Islands through the snowdrifts.

"We got home around suppertime," Otis recalls. As several of the other boats started arriving between 7:00 and 9:00 P.M., the men compared stories of the day. Only then, did they realize how fortunate they were to have made it home. One crew was forced to constantly bail water during the trip back. Their small boat sprung a leak after being battered by the heavy seas.

"The seas knocked the oakum out of her and she sank just as they got in. They just made it to the wharf," Otis remembers.

As they chatted about the storm and made other small talk, the Horse Island men kept a close watch on the harbour entrance. There were three boats from the island that still hadn't made it back to port. Bob and Purse Bath and Win Greenham was one crew still unaccounted for. While casting anxious eyes toward the sea, most men hoped that the others had been simply blown off course in the storm and had made it safely to Fleur de Lys, Coachman's Cove or some other nearby community.

Back in Wild Cove, Mark and Allan Small's family was fairly contented, thinking the brothers were safe on the Horse Islands. They were safe but not on the Horse Islands. By the time Mark and Allan reached the lighthouse, darkness was falling and they had little time to prepare for the night. Breaking the door to the unmanned lighthouse with an axe, the brothers gathered enough wood to build a fire. Although Mark was burdened by a severe stomach ailment, both men were dry and warm and enjoying a meal of canned beans just after dark.

Sunday morning dawned a fair day. Fog shrouded Harbour Deep Point but after resting and even catching a little bit of sleep on the lighthouse floor, Mark and Allan left the little lighthouse and started the five-mile trek to the fishing community of Harbour Deep. It was a hard walk. They had to climb a thickly wooded mountain to get to Harbour Deep. At approximately two o'clock in the afternoon they could see the community in the distance. But even then, the journey was not over for the two brothers. They were across the harbour from Harbour Deep and it would take several more hours to walk the shoreline and cliffs to get to the other side. Tired and weary, they decided to try another option. Perhaps someone would pick them up in boat if they could attract their attention, they thought. While Mark built a fire, Allan fired several shots from his rifle.

"It was the first time I ever fired a gun on Sunday," says Allan, a devoutly religious man. They did attract attention and by suppertime, the two brothers were resting comfortably in the homes of new friends in Harbour Deep.

Although they were fine, Mark and Allan had no way of contacting their family to inform them that they were safe. There was no phone and to makes matters worse, heavy ice had filled the harbour making it impossible to get out of the community by boat.

On the Horse Islands, word spread quickly on Sunday morning that two of the overdue boats had made it to land, but there was still no sign of Bob, Purse and Win. Because of the extremely high winds and seas on Saturday, and then a subsequent change in wind direction on Sunday, the search would have to be spread over a very large area of ocean and seashore alike. During the search, Mark and Allan's boats were found drifting in ice near Jackson's Arm. Not knowing the brothers had made it to land, the search escalated to look for five missing men instead of three.

Eventually, someone got word out that Mark and Allan Small were safe in Harbour Deep, but sadly the news was not as happy for the families of Bob and Purse Bath and their friend Win Greenham. Their boat was sighted just off Sisters Island, near Baie Verte but the three men were nowhere to be seen. The trapskiff was found floating upright, half full of water and ice, but it appeared that the 28-foot boat had not capsized. Batteries, an anchor on the cuddy in the bow, along with other unsecured items, were still in their original positions, indicating that the boat had not rolled over.

On the other hand, rifles, grub bags and a small rowboat were missing. Fishermen believe that the boat broke down or ran out of gas and the three tried to make it to land in their small lifeboat, taking their survival items such as guns and food with them. They never made it. No trace of the rowboat or the three men was ever found.

The first day of the sealing season 1962 was the *final voyage* for Bob Bath, his son Purse and Edwin (Win) Greenham.

Close Call Helps Solve a 24-Year-Old Mystery

After years wondering, Bernard Bourgeois now has a pretty good idea what happened to his brother Francis back in 1976. After a lifetime on the water, the Benoit's Cove fisherman was just months away from his sixty-fifth birthday and a long awaited retirement when he came very close to ending his career in tragedy.

On May 23, 2000, Bernard, known to everyone in the Bay of Islands as Bernie, was hauling his lobster pots just as he'd done for more than 50 years. He recalls letting go of the still-running outboard engine to start the motor on his lobster trap hauler, but before he could do that, the boat suddenly lurched to one side and as quick as a flash, Bernie was in the ocean while the boat was speeding away from him.

It was a close call, but the 64-year-old fisherman managed to swim to shore, and although dazed from the effects of hypothermia caused by spending about 20 minutes in the frigid waters of Bay of Islands, he made it to the beach, relatively alert. Bernie stumbled and staggered along the shoreline for another 20 minutes, and finally managed to reach a cabin where he found refuge. After a good rest and then a short visit to the hospital in Corner Brook, Bernie was soon fit as a fiddle once again.

Looking back at his ordeal today, Bernie thinks he knows exactly how his brother Francie (Francis) died exactly 24 years earlier in May 1976.

The Bourgeois brothers were both fishing out of Highlands Beach several miles south of Bay of Islands that spring. Tuesday, May 11, was a perfectly calm day so Francie and Bernie, along with their fishing buddies Ray and Joe Hynes, also from the Bay of Islands, decided it was a good opportunity to shift their lobster pots to new locations. All four men took to their individual dories early that morning. All through the day they hauled and shifted lobster traps, breaking occasionally to go ashore to their cabins on the beach for a snack or a few minutes rest. At approximately 3:30 P.M., Bernie brought his boat alongside his older brother's dory to chat about what they would do next. "You might as well go on in and start cooking supper for us," Francie said to Bernie, explaining that he would stay out for another hour or so.

About a half an hour later, as Bernie started to make a stew for all four fishermen, Ray Hynes was setting his last lobster trap for the day. Before heading ashore to the cabin about one and a half miles away, Ray also decided to stop by to check on his friend Francie, who still had several lobster traps piled up in his boat. Again, Francie suggested that Ray should go ashore, saying that he'd be along as soon as he finished setting the last few pots he had on board.

"I'll be in before dark," he called to Ray, who was already heading for the beach.

Back in the cabin, 41-year-old Bernie Bourgeois was busy cooking supper, but from time to time he would glance out the window keeping an eye on his brother's dory in the distance. Around 5:00 P.M., Bernie grew concerned when he noticed that Francie's small boat hadn't moved very far during the past 20 or 25 minutes.

"If Francie was setting lobster traps he should have moved on from that location by now," he said to himself, half aloud. Keeping a closer watch on his brother's dory, Bernie finally thought there might be something wrong with Francie. Worried that it would soon be dark, Bernie mentioned his concern to Ray Hynes.

"Let's get in the truck and go down the road to get a closer look," Ray said without hesitating. When the two fishermen drove out to a headland about a mile down the coastline near the spot where Francie had been setting pots, they could clearly see his dory drifting about a half mile offshore from the beach.

There was no sign of Francie.

Rushing back to their cabins, Ray and Bernie alerted several other fishermen in the area that Francie might be in trouble. Within minutes, a dozen or more fishermen in eight or 10 dories were searching the coastline, hoping to see Francie walking on the beach or swimming. Just as darkness fell over Highlands, searcher Michael Gillis discovered Francie's lifeless body floating, but tied to a lobster buoy, about one and a half miles from the spot where the fisherman is believed to have set his last lobster trap that evening.

For a little while, some of the fishermen were puzzled about why and how Francie was tethered to a buoy. Bernie says he's confident that he knows what happened. Bernie thinks his brother swam as far as he could, but the ice cold water of St. George's Bay in early May took its toll and he couldn't make it any farther. Realizing that the beach was too far away, Francie saw the buoy and tied himself to it

Bernard Bourgeois.

in the hopes that someone would find him alive, even if he lost consciousness. The rope on the buoy was very deliberately tied around his arm, according to Bernie. "It wasn't snagged. There were two neat turns around the arm just the way you'd tie a rope to anything to keep it from getting away," he explains. An experienced fisherman, Francie was also aware that if he died, it would be better for his family to find his body rather than taking a chance on being washed out to sea by the currents, never to be found.

Thinking back on his own close call last year, Bernie Bourgeois says it's almost certain that Francie wound up in the ocean the same way he did. He says that sometimes fishermen make bigger mistakes in perfect sea conditions than in bad weather because of a false sense of security that comes with working in ideal weather.

"He had to let go his motor to start his hauler just like I did, and before you know it, the engine turns and you're gone as quick as that," he explains, suggesting that if the water had been choppy, Francie might have been a little more careful. In rough weather conditions, fishermen tend to stop the motor before moving away from it.

Bernie survived his brush with death fishing from a lobster boat and lived to retire with his family in Benoit's Cove. Sadly, his brother Francie Bourgeois made his *final voyage* on May 11, 1976.

Unusual Event Causes Tragic Delay

Tuesday, October 8, 1998 was an exciting morning in Rose Blanche. Early morning risers were soon informed that they had an unusual visitor to their picturesque southwest coast community. A young bull moose had been spotted strolling around the west side of the community. If that wasn't enough to get people out of bed a few minutes earlier than usual, it seems that when the animal made up his mind to visit the eastern side of Rose Blanche, he decided to take a shortcut. Instead of walking around the horseshoe-shaped harbour, he decided to swim. Within minutes, dozens of people were lining the beach to get a better view; some even got in their boats and went out in the harbour to get a close-up look.

Wilfred Mauger, known to everyone, including his family, as Junior, was watching the activity from his fishing stage. The 32-year-old fisherman had just returned from setting six tubs of trawl lines near Petite's Buoy, about two miles from Rose Blanche. Junior usually set his fishing gear alone or "cross-handed" as they called it in that area, but he always liked a little help to haul his trawls.

Luck was with the young Rose Blanche fisherman that morning. His friend Austin Farrell was home for a few days, taking a break from longliner fishing out of Nova Scotia. On Monday night, the two friends talked about all the fishing news and, as usual, they discussed the weather and the possibility of going out fishing the next morning. Junior was eager to go because the fishing was good and he wanted as much of the small quota allocated to his area as he could catch. The forecast called for a stiff breeze from the north, but it looked like it was not going to hit the coast until late morning or noon. Junior figured that if he could get an early start and set out his gear by 6:00 A.M., he could haul before the wind struck. Austin said that he'd be happy to lend a hand, and told his friend that he'd meet him at 7:00 A.M. at Junior's fishing stage.

As the two men prepared to leave for Petite's Buoy, they were distracted by all the excitement caused by the swimming moose. Not wanting to miss out on seeing first-hand what they both knew was going to be the "conversation of the month" when they returned, the two fishermen stayed and watched the drama unfolding in the harbour. Finally, at 8:00 A.M., Junior steered his 19-foot speedboat around Cains Island and headed toward the fishing grounds. Junior knew he was a little late in leaving, but with Austin's help he figured they wouldn't be long hauling his six tubs of trawl. The weather was fine and they'd still have time to get back by noon as he promised his wife, Pam, the night before.

Pam Mauger didn't have to wait till noon to start worrying. At ten-thirty that morning she was startled by a loud noise.

"At first I thought it was a gunshot and then I realized that something must have struck the side of the house," she recalls. Going outside to investigate the source of the noise, Pam was surprised at the force of the northerly wind. It was almost as if it struck without warning.

"One minute there was nothing and suddenly it was blowing a gale," she says.

Satisfied that the noise was caused by something thrown against the house by the sudden high winds, Pam no longer cared to know what the object might have been. She had more important things on her mind. Having grown up surrounded by fishermen, Pam knew that a strong wind blowing off the land like that could cause trouble for fishermen in small open boats, especially if they had a load of fish aboard.

Although she tried to convince herself that Junior was safe, deep down Pam knew that her husband's boat was likely to be low in the water that morning. She remembered that he landed 900 pounds of cod the day before, and he mentioned that there was still a good sign of fish in the afternoon when he came in on Monday. She knew that six tubs of trawl lines along with two men and even half that amount of fish would weigh heavy on a small boat. Unable to wait until Junior's scheduled arrival time, Pam drove down the road just outside Rose Blanche to an area where she could get a view of the coastline looking toward Petite's Buoy. Seeing nothing, she walked out on the long headland leading to the Rose Blanche lighthouse to get a better look. There was still no sign of the men.

As she walked and drove between both locations, she asked several people if any of the other fishermen had mentioned seeing her husband and Austin. No one had, but someone who had obviously sensed Pam's anxiety phoned Austin's brother, Russell Farrell, and told him that Pam was very worried about her husband and his friend. Russell, a longliner fisherman who knew the danger of high winds and small boats, was soon steaming past Cains Island to look for his brother and Junior. It didn't take long to find the first clue that something had gone wrong.

Slightly relieved that help was on the way, Pam went home and tuned the VHF radio set to the channel used by fishermen. At approximately 2:00 P.M., Pam heard that Russell had found a floating buoy and requested confirmation of Junior's CFV (fishing vessel number). A few minutes later, Russell was informed that the number matched the one on the buoy he had picked up.

"That's when I knew," Pam says softly.

The agony of a long search was unnecessary. By mid-afternoon, searchers had recovered the bodies of both men, clad in flotation jackets near the trawl where their boat had been swamped. The fisherman who later completed hauling Junior's trawl lines said the men had almost finished the job that day.

"He said another ten minutes or so and they might have done it," Pam recalls.

Pam Mauger is satisfied that her husband was not negligent or careless that day. She says there were several other small boats out and the weather was fine until the sudden onslaught of a heavy wind, just as Junior and Austin were completing their work. The only nagging feeling she has today is about the moose in the harbour in the early morning. If that hadn't happened, she wonders if her husband and his friend might have finished hauling the trawls in time to get back home before the hard wind struck.

No one will ever be able to answer that question for Pam Mauger. The only thing certain is that on Tuesday, October 8, 1998, her husband, Junior (Wilfred) Mauger, and his friend Austin Farrell took their *final voyage*.

Tragic Fishing Trip Leaves Lasting Mark on Young Survivor

Calvin Pierce Jr. is doing fine now.

The 26-year-old native of Harbour Breton is married and living in St. John's. Calvin and his wife Sherry can't wait for the arrival of their first baby in March.

But, Calvin Pierce will never go fishing again even if he lives to be a hundred, not since the accident that claimed the life of his dad, Calvin Pierce Sr., and his uncle, Hughie Snook.

Friday, May 10, 1996 started out as a typically cool spring morning in Harbour Breton. Although there were patches of ice in Northeast Arm, about five miles from town, Calvin Pierce Sr. knew it was a good morning to go herring fishing. Calvin's brother, Gordon Pierce, his brother-in-law, Hughie, and his son, Calvin, decided to join the 46-year-old fisherman for the day.

Fishing was good and the four men were soon on the way back to Harbour Breton with about 3,000 pounds of herring in their 19-foot speedboat. By noon, the southeast winds had freshened a little but not much. When the four fishermen finished unloading their catch, Calvin decided that it was safe enough to go back to their bar seine and get another load. Although waves were getting higher with the strengthening wind, he figured that things would be fine as long as they didn't overload the boat. Just before 2:00 P.M., the four were again on the way from Northeast Arm to the fish plant in Harbour Breton, this time with just more than a half-boatload of herring.

Calvin Sr. kept the speedboat at a slow but steady pace as he steamed toward port on the western side of Northeast Arm in the lee of the cliffs, about a quarter mile offshore. A little over one mile into the four-mile trip back to port, a large wave struck broadside, partially filling the front fish-well with water. Herring in the boat's fish-wells shifted in the water and flushed forward to the front. With the bow just inches above water, a second wave easily washed over the gunwales, completely filling the boat.

When the speedboat began to capsize and roll over, all four men jumped into the water. Moments later, they were scrambling for safety on top of the overturned hull of the small vessel. As wave after wave swept over the boat, nearly washing the men overboard each time, Calvin Jr. decided to get into the water to try and steady the boat. Buoyed by his immersion suit, the young man managed to get the boat's painter under his feet for support as he stood in the water holding on to the stem. As each wave approached, Calvin pushed and turned the boat in a way to minimize the impact of the waves when they struck. While manoeuvring the boat, Calvin was also shedding his rubber clothes and the hip rubbers that were filled with water and dragging him down.

Realizing that the icy cold water would soon cause hypothermia, Calvin Jr. knew that something had to be done immediately. That's when he remembered the other smaller boat they had tied to the bar seine.

"I thought that if I could get that small boat, I could come back and get the other three safely to shore," he says.

Not a strong swimmer, Calvin floated on his back, and using his best imitation of the backstroke, he finally made it close enough to shore to crawl to the beach on his hands and knees.

But despite being safe on land, Calvin's worst nightmare was just beginning.

As he removed his cumbersome immersion suit in order to move more freely, Calvin glanced out over the bay and saw his three relatives still clinging to the overturned speedboat. Wearing only wool socks, Calvin couldn't run on the jagged, ice-covered, rocks but he walked as fast as he could, his feet numb from the freezing temperatures.

About halfway along the one-mile stretch of shoreline to the boat, Calvin faced a serious dilemma. The beach ended where a steep rocky cliff jutted out into the ocean. The only way to the other side was to climb over the cliff or swim around the headland. Even without boots, Calvin immediately chose to climb. On the other side of the cliff, he was faced with another obstacle. A small trench-like gorge ran from the shoreline as far inland as he could see. Covered in thick brush and trees, it was nearly impossible to walk inland to the end of the crevice. Calvin had just one option; he had to jump across the chasm. Beating down bushes and breaking tree branches with his bare hands, he made a clearing long enough to get up a running speed before jumping. Backing up as far as he could, he mustered what strength he had remaining and ran.

He almost made it.

Landing about two feet short of the top of the trench, he landed on the slanting side of the rocks.

"I remember my hands digging into the ground and pulling myself up to the top," he says.

Calvin Pierce.

Finally, Calvin reached the beach where the small boat was located about 100 feet offshore. But then he faced yet another hazard. Could he possibly swim to the boat without his floater suit to keep him safely above water? he wondered. Driven by anxiety and an overwhelming compulsion to rescue his father and his uncles, there was only one thing to do. Calvin doesn't remember the swim, but he knows he couldn't climb over the side of the small boat once he got there. Finally, he pulled himself around the gunwales to the stern where he positioned the outboard motor in a way that he could step on the propeller housing and push himself into the boat.

By the time Calvin made it back to the overturned speedboat, there was no one there. Suddenly he noticed two men floating, lifelessly near the shoreline.

"Exact details are hard to remember, but I knew by the way they were floating or something that my father and Hughie were gone; that there was no hope for them, so I turned my attention to the third person, the one I couldn't see at the time." Steering the boat around in circles, just offshore from the beach, Calvin finally caught a glimpse of his uncle lying on the rocks. Afraid the engine wouldn't start again if he shut it off, Calvin rammed the boat in on the beach as he tilted the outboard motor and left it running with the propeller out of water. Shouting and waving, Calvin was overjoyed to see Gord finally kneeling on his hands and knees.

"He was dazed and frothing from the mouth, but I grabbed his pants and pulled on him until we managed to get in the boat."

Afraid they couldn't make it all the way to Harbour Breton in the choppy seas, Calvin headed toward a cottage near the beach in Baldens Cove about half a mile away. Calvin noticed the owner of the cabin was there earlier in the day and hoped the man was still there.

Finally, Calvin's luck took a turn for the better. The owner, Stan Perry, was still at his cabin that afternoon. Calvin wolfed down a tin of Irish Stew and, leaving his uncle Gordon at the cabin with Stan, he started out on his last painful journey that day. Walking the half-mile path to the highway, the young man flagged down a passing car and hitched a ride to the RCMP station in Harbour Breton. The police officer on duty recorded the time of Calvin's arrival at the detachment headquarters as approximately 4:00 P.M.

Gordon Pierce made a full recovery, although he is still haunted by the memories of the ordeal. He continues to live in Harbour Breton. Calvin Pierce moved to St. John's and vows he will never fish for a living.

No one is absolutely sure why Calvin Pierce Sr. and Hughie Snook left the overturned boat. They may have decided that their best chance of surviving in the bitterly cold water was to try and swim to shore, or perhaps they grew too tired to hang on and were washed off the swamped hull of the speedboat. An autopsy report determined that Calvin Sr. and Hughie died by drowning on their *final voyage*.

Proper Suits and Proper Training Saved the Day

Trevor Short and his five-man fishing crew are living testaments to the effectiveness of survival (immersion) suits and safety-practice drills at sea.

Without suits and the familiarity with how they worked, some or all of the six crew members of the longliner *Atlantic Prize* would undoubtedly be dead.

On November 5, 1998, the *Atlantic Prize* had completed a routine day fishing redfish on the Grand Banks, about 200 miles southeast of St. John's. Fishing had been good and the six men had safely stowed 100,000 pounds of fish in the holds of the 65-foot longliner. By late night they were headed for port in Gaultois, on Newfoundland's south coast. Mate Trent Roberts was on watch while engineer Jeff Whyatt made a snack in the galley. The other four men decided to "turn in" and get some sleep.

At the wheel, Trent Roberts had pleasant thoughts running through his mind that night. He turned 24 that day. It was also the eve of his grandfather's birthday. Fishing had been good and the forecast looked fair for the trip to port. There was a stiff southwesterly breeze blowing and seas had increased significantly since darkness fell. But still, Trent wasn't worried. Conditions were no worse than many of the storms the *Atlantic Prize* had dealt with dozens of times before in her 10 years fishing the northwest Atlantic.

But the storm grew steadily worse and, as it did, the *Atlantic Prize* rolled significantly with the strong southwesterly winds on her port beam. About 1:50 A.M., Trent noticed the *Atlantic Prize* was "sluggish" returning upright from the starboard rolls. A few minutes later, the vessel developed a permanent list to starboard and that was when Trent knew something had gone terribly wrong. With a quick glance aft, the young but experienced mate knew they were in trouble when he saw water shipping over the deck. Running quickly to the cabin, Trent alerted Jeff in the galley and then went immediately to wake the skipper.

A little groggy but still very alert, Trevor only needed one quick look out the porthole to realize that there was no time for lengthy assessments.

Yelling to Trent, "Call the boys! Call the boys!" Trevor scurried up the steps to the wheelhouse to send a mayday. In the few seconds that it took to get a distress call clear, water had already started to fill the wheelhouse, the highest point on board the vessel.

The following two minutes accounted for the difference between life and death for Trevor, Trent, Jeff and their shipmates Rex Taylor, Matty Tobin and Josh Williams. Fortunately, the safety drills that Trevor insisted on carrying out at least six or seven times a year paid huge dividends. Without looking to see what was happening, deckhand Matty Tobin raced straight to the locker where the survival immersion suits were stowed. Meticulously following the steps he had learned from all the drills, Matty grabbed suits for all hands and started handing them out.

Training and experience would again be a crucial factor during the next few seconds, when all six men suited up in about one-tenth the time that it would take an inexperienced and untrained person. With the *Atlantic Prize* listed out at a 90-degree angle and rapidly sinking, the crew tried to ready the 10-man life raft from the vessel, but the inflatable raft got carried away from them before they could get on board. With no options remaining, the six men started jumping into the ocean before the *Atlantic Prize* sank. They all knew the undertow from the large vessel going down could drag them down with the vessel.

A minute later, the crew of the *Atlantic Prize* realized they had just embarked on their worse nightmare.

Fighting against 15-foot waves, Trevor Short swam to look for his crew members. In the distance he could hear Matty calling. A short while later, he also connected with Rex but in the darkness there was no sign of Jeff, Josh and his cousin Trent.

Bobbing around in the rough seas, Trevor noticed something that appeared different from cresting waves. Peering closely through the darkness, he saw a badly battered, but still floating, aluminum rowboat that had somehow broken free from the *Atlantic Prize* before it sank. Managing to climb on board the little boat gave the three men a ray of hope but not a great deal. There were no paddles and it was a struggle to keep emptying water from the boat with nothing but their hands to use as bailers.

As they bailed and drifted, all three kept wondering what had happened to their shipmates. At one point, an overly anxious Trevor Short jumped back in the ocean and swam to look for his missing crew members. When there was no sign of anyone, he reluctantly returned to the relative safety and comfort of the little aluminum rowboat.

Amazingly, Trent, Jeff and Josh had all managed to surface in the same area when they jumped from the *Atlantic Prize*. Without a life raft, or even pieces of debris to cling too, the three decided to link arm in arm and ride it out. With Jeff, the biggest of the three, in the middle, Trent and Josh both paddled with their one free arm to keep their backs to the oncoming waves.

"Every fifth or sixth wave would be a real big one," Trent remembers. "We could hear it roar just as it broke over us, so we'd all hold our breath and wait till you couldn't hear bubbles anymore – and then we'd try to breathe again."

To be lost overboard in the frigid northwest Atlantic Ocean on a stormy November night is every fisherman's worst fear, but still the crew of the *Atlantic Prize* insist they never once thought about dying out there. Trevor says when he saw the lights of the first search plane, he constantly talked to the others about simply waiting it out until daylight and everything would be fine.

Downwind, about three or four miles away, the other guys even joked about "this being a hell of way to get your first helicopter

Three men hanging on to an overturned boat.
Illustration by Ian Williams.

199

ride," thinking a chopper would be out to get them as soon as daylight broke.

But there was no helicopter at dawn. In fact, it never occurred to some of the men that they were too far from land and out of helicopter range, although Trevor kept telling his group that he expected one.

"I knew the difference, I was just trying to say anything to keep morale up," he says with a smile.

There were no helicopters, but there were fixed wing aircraft circling, and sometime about 7:00 A.M. the *Atlantic Dorothy*, a fishing trawler out of Marystown, appeared on the horizon, heading almost directly toward the three men in the small boat. Elation quickly turned to frustration though, when the vessel steamed past them without catching a glimpse of the men who were shouting and frantically waving their arms.

Buoyed by the knowledge that search planes and ships were in the area, everyone was confident that all they had to do was stay busy paddling to keep warm, and there would be a happy ending to this ordeal.

They were right!

At 7:30 A.M. the *Atlantic Dorothy* received word that a plane had spotted the aluminum boat with survivors on board. Armed with precise coordinates, Captain Rene Langdon carefully manoeuvred his ship alongside the small half-submerged rowboat a half-hour later.

Before his feet touched the deck of the large trawler, Trevor Short was shouting to the ship's mate that there were three more men floating somewhere in the vicinity.

"I knew they would be floating because they were suited up," he explains.

On the bridge, Captain Langdon immediately proceeded to steam toward the area where they calculated Trent, Jeff and Josh might have drifted, based on where the other three were found.

"I was sure we were looking for bodies and not survivors," says the veteran fishing captain, thinking that no one could have survived that storm without some form of shelter. Moments later he received another message from an aircraft that the three men had been sighted floating about five miles away from the *Atlantic Dorothy's* position. Even from the air, the aircraft crew could tell that the three were not only alive but, judging from their vigorous arm-waving, they were obviously doing fairly well.

When a crew member from the rescue ship went to the galley to inform Trevor, Matty and Rex that their shipmates had been sighted alive, an emotional Trevor Short laughed and cried, all the while shouting, "That's my boys! That's my boys!"

A day later, Trevor and "the boys" were safe onshore in Marystown, and although tired and weary from the longest night of their lives, not one of them had even caught a cold.

Within days of arriving back home, there was a new trawler in the planning stages. Even with the excitement of a new and more modern vessel, it will be a long time before Trevor Short, Trent Roberts, Jeff Whyatt, Rex Taylor, Matty Tobin and Josh Williams forget November 6, 1998 and the *final voyage* of the *Atlantic Prize*.

An Amazing Display of Courage by Young Kids

Kristen Whelan learned to swim in a freshwater pond near her home in Lumsden, Newfoundland.

That was in the first week of July 1997.

Little did the 13-year-old know that two weeks later her life would depend on her newly developed skills.

On Sunday, July 13, Kristen's father, Dennis Whelan, decided to put his longliner *Miss Cat Harbour* on dry dock in Musgrave Harbour to repair a cutlass bearing. After chatting with crew members Kirk Goodyear and Watson Cuff, it was decided that Kirk would skipper the boat to Musgrave Harbour the next day. The plan called for Kirk and Watson to take the boat, and while they were steaming the two-and-a-half-hour trip, Dennis would drive to Musgrave Harbour. That way, Dennis could pick up the things needed to do the repairs and then meet the others at the marine service centre.

Monday turned out to be a fine day in Lumsden. After lunch, Dennis, Kirk and Watson went on board the 34-foot longliner to get things in order for the trip. Just before Watson and Kirk were about to leave, Kristen and her friend Travis Stokes, also 13, dropped by to see what was happening. Because it was such a beautiful day, Kristen and Travis decided to stay on board the longliner and go to Musgrave Harbour for a boat ride.

Around 1:30 P.M., everything was ready. Dennis untied the boat's lines and the two men and two teens were on their way. As Dennis drove up the hill from the wharf, he felt a strange sense of uneasiness. Stopping his car, he looked back at the longliner steaming out from the harbour.

"I don't remember ever doing that before," he says. "It was like I was spooked or something."

Dennis waited until after three o'clock before leaving Lumsden, timing his estimated arrival in Musgrave Harbour to coincide with the boat's docking. Near Anchor Brook, approximately 20 kilometres from Lumsden, Dennis noticed what appeared to be a small open boat about a kilometre offshore. Thinking it was someone out for a leisurely boat-ride on such a nice day, he continued on his trip, thinking little more of it. Arriving at the wharf in Musgrave Harbour about half an hour later, Dennis was surprised to learn that his boat had not arrived yet. *They should have been here at least twenty minutes ago*, he thought. Driving up the hill from the wharf to take a look down the so-called "straight shore," Dennis remembers a feeling of panic when there was nothing to be seen.

"I felt like someone stuck a knife in me," the big burly fisherman says, fighting back tears.

Dennis Whalen's worst fears were confirmed a few hours later.

No one knows exactly what happened but when they were off Anchor Brook, shortly after three o'clock, Kirk decided to check out something on deck. Switching on the autopilot, he left the wheelhouse and stepped outside. Kristen, who was inside the wheelhouse at the time, remembers an alarm sounding a few seconds later but she didn't know what it meant. It appears the autopilot malfunctioned and quickly pulled the rudder all the way to one side, causing the vessel to topple. A few seconds later, the *Miss Cat Harbour* was bottom up.

Kirk Goodyear was the first to surface, probably because he was on deck when the boat rolled. Kristen Whelan and Watson Cuff were in the wheelhouse but managed to push, pull and swim their way through an open door and made it to the surface a few seconds later. Kirk managed to grab the slippery keel of the overturned vessel and pulled himself to safety over the stern.

Although she was not an experienced swimmer, Kristen didn't worry about her own safety and instead focused her attention on Watson, about three feet from the boat.

"Can you swim?" she called. Watson yelled back that he couldn't swim very well although Kristen thought he was doing a reason-

Miss Cat Harbour.

ably good job of keeping himself afloat as he thrashed his arms around in the water. She didn't realize that Watson was, in fact, frantically searching for his eyeglasses, rather than attempting to tread water. While swimming toward the boat, Kristen looked back at Watson and noticed that his head was barely above the surface. Realizing that Watson was in bigger trouble than she thought, Kristen decided she had to try to help, because the ocean's currents had already started driving him in the opposite direction from the overturned boat. Although she was nearly close enough to touch the vessel, Kristen turned and swam back toward Watson.

Intent on helping Watson, the young teenage girl hadn't noticed that Travis was nowhere in sight. The young fellow had gone below deck to the engine room just before the boat capsized and was trapped there. Amazingly though, the boy maintained his composure and knew that getting out of the engine room required total concentration. With water pinning him to the ceiling of the engine room, Travis realized he would have to swim downwards to the hatch before he could even get outside the boat. Mustering strength and courage he never knew he possessed, he swam straight down and deeper underwater before finally finding his way out. Gasping for air, the youth surfaced near the side of the boat in the nick of time.

Unaware that Travis was safe on the boat with Kirk, Kristen continued swimming toward Watson. Sadly, by the time she got there, Watson was floating, lifeless and face down in the water. Kristen instinctively knew there was nothing she could do.

Overwhelmed with fear and grief, Kristen was rapidly losing strength. As she turned and saw the bottom of the longliner floating about 70 feet away, she wondered if she could make it back. As she struggled to swim, Kristen could hear shouts of encouragement from Travis and Kirk, but her strongest incentive to survive came when she thought of her grandmother. Thinking that she might never see her beloved "Nan Goodyear" again, Kristen summoned every ounce of strength left in her young body to make it to the overturned vessel. When she finally got within five or six feet from the boat, Kirk removed his sweater and threw it toward her as a makeshift lifeline. Exhausted, Kristen managed to reach up from the water and grabbed the arm of the sweater as Kirk pulled her toward the stern where she climbed to safety.

For the next three hours, Kirk Goodyear and the two youths huddled on the keel of the overturned boat praying that someone would notice them.

Luckily, someone did.

Onshore, thinking that something had gone wrong, Dennis quickly drove to the home of his friend George Abbott in Musgrave Harbour. After listening to Dennis for a couple of minutes, George grabbed his binoculars as they both headed for his car. At Anchor Brook, Dennis scanned the ocean with the binoculars and within a few seconds he realized that what he earlier thought was a small open boat was in fact his own longliner bottom up.

It took a few moments before the awful truth sunk in.

"There are only three people on the bottom of the boat but there should be four of them," he said to George.

Racing back to Musgrave Harbour, George called Newman Mouland, owner of a fast cruiser-type speedboat. Within minutes, Newman and his friend Keith Abbott were speeding toward the overturned *Miss Cat Harbour*.

As the three survivors clung to the slippery bottom of the capsized longliner, their hopes of being rescued were quickly fading. Five caplin seiners passed just outside them, but no one noticed the capsized vessel because it was so low on the water. Meanwhile, around 5:30 P.M., Travis, who was coated with oil that had spilled from the engine room, was quickly becoming hypothermic and wanted to sleep. To add to their misery, the winds increased from the north causing a sudden chill in the air as the sun gave way to cloud cover and a cold mist. For most of the time they could see the lifeless body of their friend Watson Cuff still floating face down as he drifted farther and farther from them. Sometime around 5:30 P.M., he faded from their view.

As Travis became weaker, Kirk was also growing delirious in the cold. Although she was near collapsing, Kristen somehow managed to hold on, constantly encouraging the other two to hang on with her. They did until finally they heard the sounds of a motor coming toward them. As feelings of joy swept over them, all three survivors were suddenly invigorated and soon on board Newman Mouland's boat heading for Musgrave Harbour.

Young Kristen Whelan, Travis Stokes and Kirk Goodyear survived that awful day but, sadly, it was the *final voyage* for 49-year-old Watson Cuff.

Nightmare at Iron Bound, Labrador

Sandy Powell knows a lot about winds. Having spent most of his 51 years working on the Labrador Sea, the Charlottetown, Labrador fisherman has seen more than a few storms that packed a heavy wind. As a commercial pilot of single-engine airplanes for several years in Labrador, Sandy also knows a thing or two about head-winds, tailwinds and crosswinds. But for Sandy, all the other winds seem like mere summer breezes when compared to the storm of October 1975.

Sandy had mechanical problems on his 53-foot longliner, *Blanche Marie II*, that summer. After losing a significant portion of the peak fishing season due to gearbox problems, Sandy, his brother Tony Powell, Eugene Clark and Dennis Gillingham decided to steam north to the Makkovik area in late September to see if they could salvage a successful season by gillnetting codfish. The crew were keenly aware of the precarious weather systems that could quickly develop off north-ern Labrador in October, and although all the young men were in their twenties, they were careful to pay very close attention to marine weath-er forecasts for the northern Labrador coast. They also spent most nights in port at Makkovik in case they needed shelter from a sudden storm or heavy winds. By late October, seven of the nine compartments in the fishhold of the *Blanche Marie II* were filled with salted codfish.

"Another couple of hauls and we would've had them all full," Sandy says.

Sandy doesn't remember the date other than, "it was sometime in late October 1975" when the forecast called for northeast winds of 20-25 knots, gusting at times to 30-35. They were fishing near Iron Bound, a six-mile long island located about 18 miles southeast of Makkovik and nine miles offshore from Cape Strawberry. Built by Captain George Jones of Little Bay Islands, the *Blanche Marie II* was one of the most seaworthy boats ever constructed in Newfoundland, according to Sandy.

"A thirty-knot wind was nothing to bother her so we decided to tie up at the wharf at Iron Bound and wait till the wind dropped off the next day."

After tying the main lines to the wharf, the crew also tied an additional heavy rope to the island itself. Although the wharf was fairly new and solid, the 24-year-old skipper took an added precaution and dropped the vessel's two anchors. Satisfied that everything was secured even more than required, the crew bunked down for the night. While the men dozed, they were conscious that the winds and seas were steadily increasing, because their vessel heaved higher and more frantically than it would have in an ordinary 30-knot wind. Still, no one was concerned until just before daylight, when a loud bang brought all hands quickly to their feet.

"It sounded like someone shot off a twelve-gauge," Sandy recalls.

The sound wasn't from a shotgun though. They soon discovered that one of the ropes had snapped. Only then did the men realize that they were facing extreme winds and very menacing seas. As the crew rushed to batten down everything inside the vessel, Sandy started the engine just in case he needed extra manoeuvrability. By mid-morning the men could hardly believe what they were seeing. Four drums full of diesel oil blew off the wharf into the ocean. "The drums didn't wash overboard," Sandy explains, knowing that it is difficult to comprehend winds of that magnitude. "There was no water on the wharf at that time. Full drums of oil blew off the wharf." The four fishermen didn't know it then, but they were caught in the midst of a vicious storm that unexpectedly split off from a hurricane in Hudson's Bay and rapidly moved southeastward. Later, they learned that winds were clocked at 116 nautical miles an hour at the weather reporting station in Hopedale. It was likely that winds were more than 120 knots offshore at Iron Bound. In today's wind speed measurement, that translates to more than 200 kilometres per hour.

Despite documented evidence that waves reached 70 feet high in Saglek in northern Labrador and rose to 40 feet in nearby Makkovik, Sandy hesitates to describe the scene because he is afraid that people will say he is lying. However, when prompted, he does explain that at times during the day, the wind was so strong that if one of the men held on to the bow railing, the wind would lift his body from the deck and he would flap like a flag on a pole.

"Not one part of his body would be touching the boat," Sandy says. "At other times, the boat would be heeled over so far that it was easier to stand on the side of the wheel house than on the floor."

Things steadily grew worse for the crew of the *Blanche Marie II* as the day progressed. One anchor pulled free from its socket while a chain broke on the other one. The last remaining rope attached to shore snapped and for the second time that day, the men could hardly believe what they saw as they watched the wharf founder as huge waves washed over the tip of the island and pounded the structure mercilessly.

The only stabilizing force left was engine power, and for a while they managed to hang on. Sometime in the afternoon their worst fear was realized when the engine lost power. Thinking the propeller had been broken by striking a log or some other debris from the wrecked wharf, Tony Powell decided it was time to take further action. Without saying anything to his brother and shipmates, Tony, a strong swimmer who was known as fearless, grabbed a heavy rope from the bow of the vessel and jumped into the foaming seas and tried to swim to shore. Stunned by his shipmate's sudden move, Eugene Clark immediately jumped overboard behind Tony, seemingly without thinking. Intending to attach the rope to a rock and secure the boat once more, Tony soon realized that the heavy, soaked rope made it impossible for him to swim in the frothing ocean and he was forced to let the line sink to the bottom. Both Tony and Eugene made it safely to shore but they could only watch helplessly as Sandy and Dennis tried to hang on as the ill-fated longliner lurched up and down like a bucking bronc in the white foaming seas.

Afraid the vessel would be bashed into splinters if it were pushed onto rocks breaking the surface nearby, the young skipper and Dennis watched like an eagle for an opportune moment to jump. While they waited, Dennis managed to cut a dory free, but the hurricane-force winds flipped the boat in the air like a matchbox until it eventually landed in the water bottom up a hundred feet or more from the longliner. A lightweight lifeboat was also cut free, but that one flew at least a half-mile through the air before it landed in the water far offshore.

Finally, as the longliner washed across the small cove and neared a rocky point of land, Sandy and Denis knew that it was now or never to make their move.

"I don't remember how me and Dennis got ashore but we managed it somehow," Sandy says.

As the *Blanche Marie II* drifted aimlessly down the Labrador coastline, Sandy and Tony Powell, Eugene Clark and Dennis Gillingham were exhausted, but they were all safe on land and surprisingly in reasonably good condition.

However, their nightmare had only just begun.

After all day and night battling raging winds of over 200 kilometres per hour, combined with seas the height of a four-storey building, Sandy Powell, his brother Tony along with crew members Eugene Clark and Dennis Gillingham were finally safe on the beach of Iron Bound Island. Shipwrecked on an uninhabited rocky island located about 18 miles southeast of Makkovik in a ferocious October storm is no picnic, but considering their nearly 24-hour struggle to survive, the men were thankful to be alive and on land.

As the winds showed no sign of abatement, the men knew that this six-mile-long island would be their home for at least a couple of days, if not longer. Sandy's first thoughts of survival turned to finding food and shelter. He knew there were several small cabins on the island where they might find refuge from the storm, but finding food was going to be a challenge, especially in winds that made even standing upright difficult and, at times, impossible.

The instinct to gather food quickly might explain why Sandy nearly jumped into the ocean when he saw a whole bologna floating just off the beach of Iron Bound Island. Had Dennis not restrained his skipper, yelling to him that it would be certain death to get into the foaming ocean, Sandy might have attempted to get what he figured would have been one full meal for all four men.

As darkness fell, Sandy and Dennis joined Tony and Eugene on the other side of the cove and started up the hill on Iron Bound Island to look for a cabin. Still stunned by an image from earlier that afternoon, when a cabin was plucked from its foundation by the extreme winds and flew through the air, finally landing in the Labrador Sea, the men were not sure what to expect as they climbed the island's east end.

"That cabin was about twenty-by-thirty feet and it flew through the air like it was made of cardboard," Sandy says.

Fortunately, not all the cabins were torn from their footings. Taking shelter in the one that looked the sturdiest, the four fishermen found wood and lit a fire in the old-fashioned pot-bellied wood stove.

Just when they thought the worst was over, a loud creaking noise told the men they would soon once again have to do battle against the raging windstorm. Unable to withstand the ferocious onslaught of winds, the cabin started to cave in on them. At grave risk of being, literally, blown off the island, they had no choice but to try and reinforce the building. Gathering rocks and all the wood and old lumber they could find, the men worked frantically and built a makeshift fortress around the cabin. Finally, they were able to rest for a while.

The warmth of the wood-burning stove was welcome relief but hunger pangs soon reminded the men that their fight to survive hadn't allowed them time to eat at all that day. The momentary respite also allowed enough time to assess their physical conditions. Dennis realized that he had a fairly serious gash on his leg, accidentally slashed by his knife, it seems, when he was struggling to cut a lifeboat free. Eugene had injured a hand on an anchor chain and ironically, Tony, who was injury-free when he arrived at the cabin, wound up with a burnt hand. The younger Powell brother had been drying his wet clothes near the stove when the warmth made him drowsy. Falling asleep for a minute, his hand dropped onto the red-hot stove, causing a fairly severe burn.

After assessing their conditions and their surroundings, the men discovered that the only thing in the cabin was a bag of sugar. Attempting to restore some energy to their tired bodies, they drank several mugs of hot water mixed with the sugar.

The instinct to survive was greater than the need to rest or eat that night, and soon the foursome were once again outside clinging on to whatever they could find while trying to build an outdoor fire. They figured that there wouldn't be any ships nearby to rescue them in this storm and, even if there were ships in the vicinity, landing on

214

Iron Bound Island would be impossible. However, they hoped and prayed that building a fire at the top of a hill might attract the attention of someone on land who would pass the word on to possible rescuers. Sadly though, they also realized that the fierce northeast wind blew the smoke out to sea in the opposite direction.

If winds had subsided at all by dawn, it was not apparent to the four stranded fishermen. But even in the continuing storm, daylight meant they could search for food. One of them found a piece of polar bear meat in an old fishing stage. It wasn't very appetizing but it was food.

"You couldn't stay in the cabin when the boys were cooking it, the smell was that bad," Sandy laughs. Someone else found a couple of rotting cod's heads that had washed ashore. Although a couple of the men ate the fish heads, Sandy said he couldn't get past the sand and grit in them.

"I decided I'd rather starve to death," he says.

On the third day, the winds and seas had finally diminished. While two men kept constantly stoking the fire on the hill, someone found a few berries to eat, while another found a hook and line and then built a small raft so they could go out and try to jig a fish.

Even the fish seemed to have no pity. After several hours jigging, the only things they caught were two small rockcods. Under normal dining conditions, rockcod is not a fish of choice, but those two had been barely warmed in water before the half-starved men devoured them.

Back home in Charlottetown, Labrador, Sandy and Tony's mother was worried about her sons. Although they didn't phone home often when they were away, she thought they would call to assure her that they were safe after such a bad storm. When there was no word from her boys, she called a family friend in Makkovik to ask if he'd look for them. Bert Winters knew that his friends had been fishing near Iron Bound Island and immediately headed in that direction.

"We saw the boat coming but, by that time, we were not sure of anything anymore – it looked like it was starting and then stopping again," Sandy recalls. "Some fellas would say 'there it is again' and we'd get right excited and then someone else would say 'nah, there's no boat out there, we're seeing things. And then we get real quiet again.'"

Sighting the smoke on the top of Iron Bound Island, Bert Winters knew that somebody was there. Because he couldn't see a vessel in the cove, he became extremely anxious when he saw only two men coming down to the shoreline to meet him. Thinking that perhaps the other two had gone down with the longliner, Bert was almost speechless, according to Sandy. The Makkovik fisherman was relieved to hear that the other two were still piling wood on the fire in case he hadn't seen them.

"The first thing we noticed was Bert's lunch bag," Sandy says. "We were like a pack of dogs when he opened it."

Back in Makkovik, Uncle Jim and Aunt Susie Anderson cared for the shipwrecked men for two days. After regaining their strength, the four hitched a plane ride to Goose Bay where they headed to the harbour to catch the CN coastal boat to Charlottetown. But even after their ordeal, the men still had one more challenge to face. The purser on the coastal boat refused to allow them to sail unless they paid for their passage up front. He wouldn't change his mind, even after their explanation of being shipwrecked, losing everything, including their cash.

Only after Tony and Denis threatened to make crab bait out of him did the purser call the ship's captain. The captain was more understanding than the purser and agreed to let them sail, but only after arrangements had been made with a Social Services office to pay for the tickets in the event the men reneged on their responsibility to pay. Sandy laughs when he tells that story today, but he recalls being angry then about having to endure that grief in light of the nightmare they had just been through.

In the end, the only thing that really matters is that Sandy Powell and his brother Tony Powell, Eugene Clark and Denis Gillingham survived one of the worst storms of the century on the Labrador coast – one that could have easily made that trip in October 1975, their *final voyage*.

"Will You Be Back for Dinner or Will I Cook Dinner for Supper?"

Jacob (Jake) Hillier looked and talked a lot like his Irish ancestors. The ruddy-faced redheaded fisherman always had a smile for anyone who would bid him the time of day, and if he had been paid 50 cents for half the codfish he gave away, he might have been a millionaire. But Jake was not a rich man, although he was happy with his comfortable modest home on Southside Road in St. John's, where he and his wife, Olive, raised nine children. Jake was contented as long as there was enough money to keep a full pot of soup on the stove. If there was any spare change left over after Olive bought groceries, Jake would enjoy a bottle of beer before supper and a quick shot of rum just before bedtime every night.

Like most fishermen in the southern areas of Newfoundland, Jake Hillier left his longliner in the water year-round. Even if the harbour froze over, large ships transiting the busy port always kept a channel open. Winter was always a good time to hunt seabirds to bring home for supper.

On Saturday, January 10, 1976 Jake and some of his friends were planning a quick trip the following morning to hunt turrs. Jake had two new guns and he was anxious to try them out. So were his sons, Tom and Perry. Sixteen-year-old Perry persuaded his older brother that it would be best if only one of them went. That way, the brothers wouldn't be arguing about who got to use the new gun. Tom, who was suffering from a cold, agreed and decided that it might be a good idea for his younger brother to take the trip, saying that he'd go later when he was feeling better. By late Saturday night, Ray Green and Eric Saunders, the two friends who also had expressed interest in going on the trip, decided that they couldn't make it either.

When Jake woke early Sunday morning, there was no doubt about what he wanted to do. It was a perfect morning. The sun was shining brightly and there wasn't a draft of wind. Jumping out of bed in eager anticipation of a morning on the water, Jake leaned over and kissed his six-year-old daughter, Lisa, who slept in the bedroom with her parents that night.

"See ya, Bun," he whispered, calling her by his nickname for the youngest of the Hillier children.

Jake then woke Perry, and the father and son were soon ready to head for the harbour.

"Will you be back for dinner or will I cook dinner for supper?" Olive called, smiling as her husband and son were putting on their jackets.

"Nah, we'll be back for dinner around twelve or twelve-thirty. 'Tis a grand day on the water sure," Jake replied with a confidence gained from more than 30 years fishing and hunting seabirds.

By 8:00 A.M., 52-year-old Jake Hillier and his son were steaming through The Narrows of St. John's Harbour in Jake's 38-foot long-liner, *Port Kerwin*. The boat was Jake's pride and joy according to Olive.

"He treated her like a baby," she often laughed.

Jake fully anticipated a good hunting day as he steered the boat towards Cape Spear, just over a mile to the southwest. With the sun glistening off the winter water, it would be easy to spot and retrieve birds that morning.

Back home at 315 Southside Road, Olive decided that she might as well start preparing for Sunday dinner since she was already up.

Glancing out the window from time to time, Olive was pleased to see that the weather remained as perfect as it was at seven o'clock that morning. *They won't be long now*, she thought to herself as she prepared dinner. When there was no sign of Jake and Perry at 12:30 P.M., Olive decided to go ahead and feed the children, but she would wait for her husband and son before sitting down for her own Sunday dinner.

As the children finished eating, Olive started cleaning dishes while keeping a constant watch out the window, expecting to see Jake and Perry coming across the road at any minute. With weather conditions still ideal, there was no compelling reason to worry about the two but, still, Olive felt a nagging sense of uneasiness. Her husband was usually on time, but thinking that perhaps the birding was

(l-r) Sam Hillier, Lisa Hillier.

either worse or better than Jake anticipated, she reasoned he must have decided to spend an extra hour on the water.

At two o'clock Olive was suddenly overwhelmed by an eerie sense of fear.

"Something has gone wrong. Jake and Perry are in trouble," she said out loud to herself. Oddly, her son Tom was also alarmed by a strange sensation of impending doom at practically the same time. Tom, who lived next door, was still battling a bad cold, but he knew that whatever he felt at that moment had nothing to do with a cold or a flu.

The disappearance of Jake and Perry Hillier is one of the strangest cases ever known to local authorities and fishermen. There was never a trace of anything found to indicate what might have happened. There was no debris, no oil slick, and there were no bodies ever seen. It was not as if the boat was out in the mid-Atlantic and had gone down in a vicious storm.

The father and son would have hunted that day in a very small radius from Cape Spear to the nearby Freshwater Bay area. The water was calm and debris would have been easy to spot even from nearby hills. Even if the engine broke down, Jake had plenty of rope on his anchors to keep them from drifting. In fact, Jake often said that as long as fishermen carried an anchor and plenty of rope, they had nothing to worry about.

The 38-foot vessel was fairly new and in good condition and carried a 12-and-a-half-foot dory as a lifeboat. They had 100 gallons of fuel on board, and although the two didn't bring any food from home, they had fishing gear and two new guns, along with two boxes of ammunition. Equipped with the propane stove that Jake carried on the boat, they could have survived for weeks on fish and seabird meat.

Perhaps the most puzzling thing of all was the fact that none of the fishing "balloons" were ever sighted. Balloons are large inflated, heavy rubber/plastic balls used as flotation devices on fishing nets. Considered as practically unsinkable, the 25 marked balloons that Jake had tied to the stern railing would have kept a large portion of the boat afloat if it had been cut down and broken in pieces by another vessel. Even if the boat sank quickly, it is believed that the balloons would have eventually worked free from the railing and surfaced within weeks. None were ever seen.

There are only questions, and lots of them, about the loss of the *Port Kerwin*. There are still no answers. Jake's son Sam still fishes in the area where his father and brother were last seen. Even now, 27 years later, Sam still wonders if he will see something on the fishing grounds that will give him a clue to what happened. The only thing for certain is that on January 11, 1976 Jake and Perry Hillier made their *final voyage.*

A Little Help from "Jackie Lantern"

Lambert Strowbridge lived for 85 years. But, it's a miracle the Placentia Bay man made it past 20.

Two months after his nineteenth birthday in 1939, Lambert and his younger sister Mary left their home on Woody Island, Placentia Bay to go to nearby Sound Island. Lambert's chore was to get groceries and other provisions for their family, but Mary was to be dropped in a cove called Muddy Hole on the north end of the island. Her job that day was to make hay from freshly cut grass. The light northwesterly breeze filled the three sails on Lambert's 20-foot punt that August morning, and in less than an hour Mary was scrambling over the beach in Muddy Hole ready to start work. Meanwhile, Lambert headed his little sailboat to the southern end of the island where the store was located.

In the late afternoon, Mary went to the hill to see if Lambert was on his way to pick her up. There was no sign of her brother. Staring down at the rocky shores of Sound Island, Mary felt drowsy after a long hard day making hay. When there was no sign of her brother, Mary lay down on a stack of hay and fell asleep.

When she woke Mary became frightened. It was now much later than the hour that Lambert said he would be there to get her but there was still no sign of him. All alone on the tip of Sound Island, Mary became concerned and started yelling for help. Luckily, the wind carried her cries all the way across to Woody Island where George

Lockyear, a teenage boy just a little older than Mary, heard her call. A short while later Mary was on her way home to safety with the young man who would later become her husband.

Lambert, however, would not get home until much later.

After dropping Mary in Muddy Hole at 10:00 A.M., Lambert had smooth sailing toward the other end of Sound Island. While a fresh breeze was blowing off the land, the sun glistened off Placentia Bay. Lambert Strowbridge was having a great time.

Suddenly, Lambert's idyllic world came to an end. Without warning, the winds changed and before he knew what had happened, a sudden squall overwhelmed the three small sails, and the punt heeled hard to the starboard side. Although Lambert fought to bring the small boat "around to the wind," the ballast of bricks and pig iron shifted and the boat flipped over.

"She went straight out on her side, with the two sails flat on the water. The jib broke off and was gone altogether," Lambert recalled.

As water gushed into the punt, Lambert scrambled to the only dry place remaining. As the little sailboat settled in the water, a small portion of the decked bow of the punt (cuddy) remained above the surface. With barely enough dry area to kneel on, Lambert climbed up on the bow and clung to the wooden hull with his fingernails.

For a while, Lambert tried to figure out a way to manoeuvre the boat toward land, but with 95 per cent of the hull underwater, the stiff breeze and strong tides easily overpowered the efforts of the teenager. There was nothing he could do but cling to the small piece of floating hull, and pray that he would soon drift ashore or be sighted by a passing boat.

Kneeling there like a cat ready to pounce on its prey, Lambert was surprised at the speed the punt was moving with the currents. On two or three occasions, he was almost close enough to a cod net to grab a buoy but since he was moving out the bay so rapidly he thought it would be just a short while before he'd make it to shore.

He was wrong.

As darkness fell, Lambert had floated more than 10 miles around Placentia Bay, and although he had been close to land several times, his hopes were constantly dashed when the currents pushed the boat away from the rocks again. Not a good swimmer, Lambert knew he needed to be very close to land before he would give up the security of the little bit of dry hull that had become his haven.

Although darkness would have dampened the spirits of most people in that situation, Lambert says he had no fear that night.

Unless you count the first time he was visited by the Jack O'Lantern, the unexplained light that appears (to this day) on Placentia Bay in the area where a ship sank in the 1800s.

"I saw it appear in the distance, and then it came toward me and stopped no more than five feet away from me," he says. Staring into the light, Lambert remembered the hundreds of stories he'd heard from the old timers on Woody Island as they talked about the strange phenomenon they called "Jack O' Lantern" or "Jackie Lantern." He even saw a mysterious light in the area himself several times, usually while a storm was brewing. According to the legend, the "Jackie

Lantern" would come on board a vessel without lights and somehow cause the boat to sink.

And that's what really scared Lambert that night. Crouching there on the submerged punt, he thought the light would somehow cause his demise. But he was pleasantly surprised. Instead of harming him, the light just shone and did nothing more.

"It was real bright," he says. "I could see the sails underwater and everything just as plain as day."

In a way, the mysterious light was a comfort to Lambert that night. As the light appeared from time to time, he felt that someone was looking out for him, that he wasn't all alone drifting aimlessly around Placentia Bay.

Maybe someone or something was looking out for him. The night sky remained clear and dawn broke a beautiful day. With the morning sun warming his soaked clothing, Lambert again felt a surge of confidence that he would make it to land on the east side of the bay.

"I kept thinking that I'd end up in Argentia," he says.

After drifting back and forth alongside several islands, Lambert finally started to float across to the east side of Placentia Bay. Once, a small schooner sailed past him, but with the wind carrying his shouts in the opposite direction, no one heard his calls for help. Several men from the community of Little Harbour saw him, but thinking it was a tree floating on the bay, they did nothing.

Finally, sometime in the afternoon, land loomed several hundred feet in front of Lambert. Hungry, thirsty, cold and very tired from clinging to a piece of wood for nearly 30 hours, Lambert was elated. Seeing a freshly painted yellow dory anchored at the base of a cliff, he was certain he would drift close enough to jump on board. As he drifted closer and closer to the dory, he prepared to make a leap. Suddenly, just when he was almost close enough to jump, the dory disappeared.

"There was no dory – it was just in my mind," he says. Although delusional from the ordeal, Lambert did float to land where he managed to scramble from the boat and wade ashore on a small beach just south of Little Harbour.

After climbing up the 100-foot cliff he started the two-mile trek to Little Harbour. Along the way he saw a small shack at the edge of a marsh. Seeing the late afternoon sun shining through the windows, Lambert felt that finally he could rest. With any luck there would be food in the shack too, he thought. As he stumbled along the path toward the shack with the sun's rays streaming through the windows, Lambert was filled with thoughts of a bunk to lie on, food to eat and most of all, water to drink. But, like the bright yellow dory an hour earlier, the shack suddenly disappeared. Unable to figure out what happened, Lambert trudged along a path until he finally reached Richard Hann's house in Little Harbour.

After drinking what Lambert says seemed like gallons of water, he was soon on the way to the comfort of his home on Woody Island. Without as much as a runny nose from his two days and one night bobbing around in the cold Atlantic Ocean, Lambert was back on the water again the next day.

Lambert Strowbridge spent many more years making a living from the land and from the sea around Placentia Bay. That day in August 1939, was the last time he ever saw his Sound Island punt, but the young man from Placentia Bay was far from taking his *final voyage*.

Dream Foretells Tragedy

Earl Poole Jr. had a strange dream on Monday night, August 10, 1992. On Tuesday morning, while waiting for Eric Belleveau to pick him up to go to work, Earl kept playing the dream sequences over and over in his mind. A few minutes later, Earl even related his dream to his boss as they drove toward their construction work-site in Halifax.

"I dreamt that I was back home in Murray's Harbour, Labrador," he said to Eric. "Dad was walking down the hall in the house with a beer in each hand, one for himself and one for me. His bottle was full of beer but when he handed me my bottle, mine was full of ashes."

Although the dream was more vivid than any dream he'd ever had, Earl Poole Jr. was not frightened by it. He loved having a beer with his dad, and it wouldn't be totally out of character for the senior Poole to do something crazy like filling a beer bottle with ashes.

The older Earl Poole was a known practical joker who loved to pull a "fast one" on his sons sometimes. But still, there was something different about this dream. There was an uncommon sense of realism that kept Earle thinking about it all day from the minute he woke up that morning.

About the same time that Earl Poole Jr. was relating his dream to his boss in Halifax, his mother, Eliza Poole, heard a knock on her door in Murray's Harbour, Labrador. *Who can that be at this hour of the morning?* she wondered.

The Pooles spent their winters in Fox Harbour-St. Lewis about 12 miles to the south, but in spring, the family packed their things and spent their summers fishing out of Murray's Harbour. There were only a couple of other families in the harbour and nobody ever dropped by for a visit early in the morning. Just as she was about to start walking toward the door to see who was knocking, something stopped Eliza from moving any farther. Certain that she heard her husband calling to her, she suddenly felt uneasy and stopped dead in her tracks.

It was only an hour earlier that Eliza watched Earl's 18-foot boat speeding out the harbour. Earl Poole, along with his son Ed and his nephew Wallace Poole, had left for Crow Bay, four miles away, to haul a caplin net. Eliza knew there was no way the men had returned, because she would have heard or seen the boat coming back. Instead of going to the door, Eliza glanced out the window. There was no sign of the boat in the harbour and neither was there any sign of her husband or Ed and Wallace.

And there was no one at her doorstep.

Trying to convince herself that she merely imagined hearing Earl's voice, Eliza returned to preparing breakfast for the men, although she couldn't dismiss a nagging feeling that something was wrong. Glancing out the window towards the ocean again, she grew even more anxious. The northwest winds had strengthened and the waves had become much higher than they were an hour before.

"I wish they had listened to me this morning," she said to herself. Concerned about winds that were already brisk and a forecast that predicted even stronger gusts as the day progressed, Eliza suggested that the men stay home and wait till the winds dropped.

"Nah, it's not that bad sure," Earl replied, already pulling on his rubber boots. "The net is only a few minutes away. By the time you have breakfast ready, we'll be back."

Breakfast time had long passed but there was still no sign of the men. Eliza kept busy around the house, constantly glancing out her window toward Crow Bay. With the bright sunshine glistening off the water, she remembers thinking that it was a pretty sight that morning, but the thing she wanted to see most was missing. There were no boats to be seen.

By late morning, the 56-year-old mother of seven couldn't stand it any longer. During her more-often-than-usual glances outside that morning, Eliza saw her neighbour, Tom Holley painting his house. Singing out to Tom from her front doorstep, Eliza explained that she was worried about her husband and the others and wondered if Tom would check on them.

Sensing Eliza's unusual anxiety, Tom wasted no time in getting to his speedboat and headed for Crow Bay.

A veteran fisherman, Tom Holley knew exactly where to look for the three men. Thinking that Earl probably had engine trouble, Tom kept a watchful eye in all directions. The 52-year-old fisherman's many years of experience told him that the wind and ocean currents that day would have moved a speedboat offshore from the bay if the engine had failed.

Manoeuvring his speedboat between the strings of mid-summer icebergs that dotted the coastline near Murray's Harbour, Tom noticed a red object floating more than half a mile offshore from Crow Bay. At first he thought it was a flotation device used to mark nets, known to fishermen as a balloon. Tom soon realized the object was a gas tank.

Sighting the gas tank raised serious concerns for Tom. Only a few minutes later, Tom Holley's worst fears were realized. In the distance he saw the overturned hull of Earle Poole's speedboat. For a brief moment Tom was elated when he saw heads bobbing in the waves near the front of the overturned vessel. "They're fine then," he said to himself. But all too soon, his elation turned to heartbreak. As he pulled his speedboat alongside, Tom saw 27-year-old Ed Poole clinging to the stem of the capsized boat with one hand and holding his father's lifeless body with the other. Ed was very weak but still alive. Earl Poole was not breathing. There was no sign of Wallace.

It wasn't easy, physically or emotionally, but Tom, a strong man, managed to pull the lifeless body of his good friend aboard the 20-

foot fibreglass speedboat first, and then he helped Ed on board. Although he was in an advanced state of hypothermia, Ed managed to tell Tom where the boat capsized – the place where he last saw Wallace. After a quick search of the area produced no sign of the missing 26-year-old man, Tom knew he had to get Ed to Murray's Harbour quickly before his condition worsened.

Despite spending nearly three hours in the cold Labrador waters, Ed Poole was soon well enough to explain what happened. The three had been pulling a net that was full of caplin. With the combined weight of the three men and the pull of the heavy net against the speedboat, the boat was drawn very low in the water. Eager to get the full load of caplin on board, nobody noticed the saltwater sloshing in over the counter (stern) of the small boat. When someone shouted that the boat was filling with water, all three moved as quickly as they could toward the front, but it was too late. Another wave washed over the stern and the speedboat capsized, throwing the three men into the ocean.

Although they were only 70 or 80 feet from the shoreline, neither Earl nor Wallace wore life jackets and neither of them could swim. Ed was wearing a floater jacket that his father insisted he'd wear that morning. Although he was once a swimmer, the young man had been suffering from a physically debilitating disease that adversely affected his motor skills. The best he could do now was to hang on. He grabbed his father but Wallace was out of reach.

RCMP divers recovered the body of Wallace Poole the next day, very near where Ed last saw him slip beneath the surface.

Miraculously, Ed Poole survived. Investigating officers noted that most people would have died from hypothermia after an hour in the cold Labrador Sea. They estimated Ed was in the water for about three hours. Sadly for 59-year-old Earl Poole and 26-year-old Wallace Poole, August 11, 1992 was the day of their *final voyage.*

Launched Stem First

Max Day was a highly respected fisherman in Portugal Cove. The 48-year-old inshore fisherman was so at home in a boat that most people joked that he must have been born in one.

One of his colleagues said, "Max was so 'catty' he could walk the gunwales of a speedboat in a nor'easter." Max's nephew, Alex Day, said that of all the fishermen in the Cove, no one thought that anything could ever happen to Max Day.

But something did happen. On Saturday, April 20, 1985, Max and his 28-year-old son, also named Max, were up bright and early, itching to set their lobster pots. The season officially opened the day before but the weather was blustery, and although the lobster grounds were just a short distance away, they couldn't take a chance going out with a load of pots or "cages" as they call them in the Cove. Their small open speedboat was not considered a match for rough water.

But Saturday was a different story.

"It was flat calm," said Max's long-time friend and sometimes fishing partner, Stuart Mitchell. Several fishermen were preparing to head out as the two Day fishermen left at approximately 6:00 A.M. Neil Mitchell was one of them. Neil helped throw the last few cages on board Max's boat before starting to load his own.

"I was probably the last one to ever speak to them," Neil says. But as ideal as it was when they left Portugal Cove, the weather soon changed for the worse. A stiff northeasterly breeze suddenly came up and the seas became choppy.

Men and lobster pots thrown overboard.
Illustration by Ian Williams.

Like some of the other fishermen, Neil and Stewart Mitchell decided to hold off from loading pots for a while and see if the winds would subside. They didn't and as the weather worsened, fishermen like the Mitchells began to worry about the Days. Around 8:00 A.M., Neil Mitchell, knowing that his friend should have been back by then, called Alex Day and expressed his concern that something might have gone wrong with Alex's uncle and cousin. Meanwhile, Neil and another fisherman, Roger Hammond, boarded Roger's boat and went out to see if there was any sign of the two men. There wasn't any sign of the fishermen but they did see their boat floating, bottom up.

"We saw the bad news," is the way Neil put it.

There had been a light snowfall the night before and, hopeful that Max Sr. and young Max had made it to shore, Neil and Roger searched the shoreline for footprints in the snow. There were none.

After the authorities were notified an official search was soon started. It wasn't long before someone sighted a red rubber work-glove about six or seven feet below water, almost directly under the overturned speedboat. A closer look revealed that the glove belonged to the younger Max. It was soon obvious that the younger of the two had become entangled in the ropes and drowned. It appeared he was attempting to reach surface by climbing the very rope he was tangled in but couldn't make it. Divers soon discovered the same fate had befallen the older Max. His body was also tangled in the ropes about 10 or 12 feet below his son.

Portugal Cove fishermen talked about that day for a long time afterwards, trying to figure out exactly what happened. Max's wife,

Sadie, still wonders if her husband fell or stumbled because he had been complaining about a bad knee for several weeks before the accident. Fishermen figure a wave caused the capsizing, but why the men drowned is a different question. Lobster fishermen in the "Cove" always set their traps in a manner similar to the way trawl lines are set. They attach 20 "cages" or pots with rope about 10 fathoms apart. When the boat capsized, it is thought, the cages fell out, but not all of them went to the bottom. The 200 fathoms of rope became tangled in the boat as well as around the two fishermen. Alex Day said there was no way they could free themselves, because the rope was tangled in lobster traps below them, as well as being snagged in the overturned boat above them. Stewart Mitchell said the rope was tangled in the boat so tightly that "not one fishermen in the Cove could untangle it – they had to cut it off."

There's an old superstition as part of Portugal Cove folklore that you never launch your boat stem first. Alex Day remembers his Uncle Max, in a hurry, launching his boat for the lobster season that year head first. That may not have had anything to do with the tragedy, but you won't ever catch Alex Day taking a chance on tempting fate by launching a boat stem first. "I don't want to push my luck any further than I have too," Alex laments today, remembering the *final voyage* of his uncle and cousin in April 1985.

"Almost Home"

On Tuesday, October 4, 1994 Pat Coady from St. John's and his four-man crew of Mark Traverse, Edward Barry, Wayne Giles and Gerald Goldsworthy spent the afternoon and early evening preparing for a two-week fishing trip. The plan was to fish turbot for a couple of days, and depending on how that went, they might also try their hand at tuna fishing on the Virgin Rocks about 100 miles southeast of St. John's. After fishnets and supplies were all safely stowed, the 45-foot *Patrick and Elizabeth* steamed out from Bay Bull's harbour at 7:30 P.M., heading for fishing grounds known as Tobin's Point, 125 miles to the northeast.

After hauling their nets once, the crew set them out again and because turbot did not appear to be plentiful, the skipper decided to steam south to the Virgin Rocks. He had two bluefin tuna left on his annual quota and this would be an opportunity to try his luck while his turbot nets soaked.

After an unsuccessful effort fishing for tuna, the *Patrick and Elizabeth* left the Virgin rocks on Monday, October 10, and steamed back to the turbot grounds on Tobin's Point. Although they had only landed slightly more than 7,000 pounds of turbot, about 20 per cent of her normal capacity, Pat Coady heard a weather forecast that made him decide to cut the trip short and head for home on Wednesday morning, October 12.

The forecast called for winds to increase to storm force Northerlies that night, and true to his reputation as a safety-conscious skipper, Pat knew that a strong northerly gale in October packed a lot of punch, and the prudent thing to do was to head for port.

The trip was relatively uneventful for most of Wednesday. Pat called his wife, Elizabeth, via radiotelephone at three o'clock in the afternoon to say that, although the weather was still nice where they were located at the time, they were on the way home because of the impending high winds. Pat was comforting to his wife, assuring her that they would be in lee of the land by the time winds reached storm force. Even if the storm struck while they were still offshore, Pat, a 20-year veteran skipper, knew what to do. As Pat explained that they would lie-to and ride out the storm if the weather got bad, Elizabeth felt reassured that everything was going to be fine, although she asked her husband to contact her again if the weather worsened.

Pat Coady.

Although the weather continued to deteriorate in St. John's, Elizabeth was relaxed. Nonetheless she was relieved when Pat called again at ten o'clock on Wednesday night. Again, her husband's confidence was comforting for Elizabeth. Although the winds were strong, probably between

40 to 50 knots by Pat's estimation, he said the seas were still not high and things were fine.

"We're only forty to fifty miles off and we'll be in port in about six or seven hours, likely about six o'clock tomorrow morning," he said.

Because of her confidence in her husband's ability to handle storm situations like he'd done many times before, Elizabeth was again reassured. After all, they were almost home, she thought as she prepared for bed.

Confident or not, Elizabeth Coady grew very concerned when there was no word from her husband by seven o'clock Thursday morning. She contacted the operator of the Bay Bulls fish plant to see if he had any news of her husband and his crew. He didn't. Because the storm was then raging, Elizabeth, her son Pat, and the local fish plant manager decided it was time to alert the Canadian Coast Guard. At 9:35 A.M., search and rescue operations were getting underway.

Because there was no mayday reported from the *Patrick and Elizabeth*, there was hope for the family and friends. Perhaps, they reasoned, the vessel's electronic systems became disabled in the storm and there was no way the crew could make contact. Maybe the longliner was riding out the storm and jogging into the gusts until winds and seas abated. There were many reasons to hope while searchers looked for the *Patrick and Elizabeth* both from the air and by ship.

Shortly after five-thirty Thursday evening, those hopes quickly grew dim. An aircraft spotted wreckage that was shortly afterwards identified as that of the missing longliner.

There was no sign of any of the five-man crew.

There is no way of knowing exactly what happened because there were no survivors to tell the tale, but whatever it was, it must have happened quickly. A life raft was recovered and found to be in good condition and operational but there was no indication the raft had been occupied. Because there is no evidence to suggest the vessel collided with any other ship, the Transportation Safety Board investigation concluded that:

> Examination of recovered debris indicated that the vessel was lost as a result of sudden catastrophic structural failure and disintegration in severe storm conditions.

Sadly, for Skipper Pat Coady, Mark Traverse, Edward Barry, Wayne Giles and Gerald Goldsworthy, what was expected to be a routine fishing trip turned out to be their *final voyage*, on Thursday, October 13, 1994.

*Memorial erected to the memory of Pat Coady and the crew of the **Patrick and Elizabeth**.*

"There are few areas in the world which possess as severe environmental conditions as the continental shelf off eastern Canada. Nowhere else are the combinations of wind, wave, fog and ice as perilous and unpredictable as in that vast and varied expanse of ocean."

> – The Royal Commission on the *Ocean Ranger*

Those perilous conditions have caused the sinking and loss of hundreds of Atlantic Canadian fishing vessels with enormous loss of life.

Well-known journalist and former CBC Radio *Fisheries Broadcast* host Jim Wellman recounts many of these gripping tales in his latest book, *Final Voyages*.